Welcome to your body

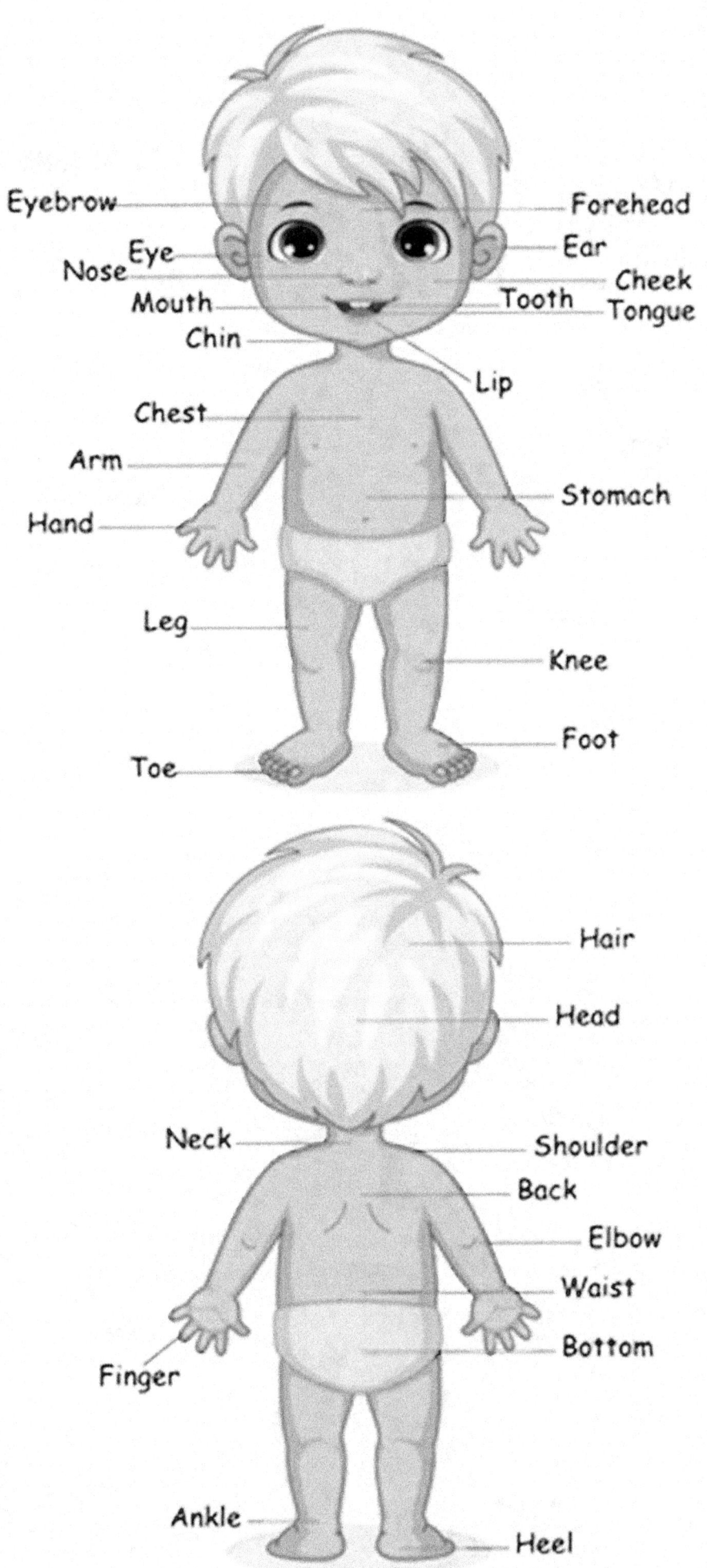

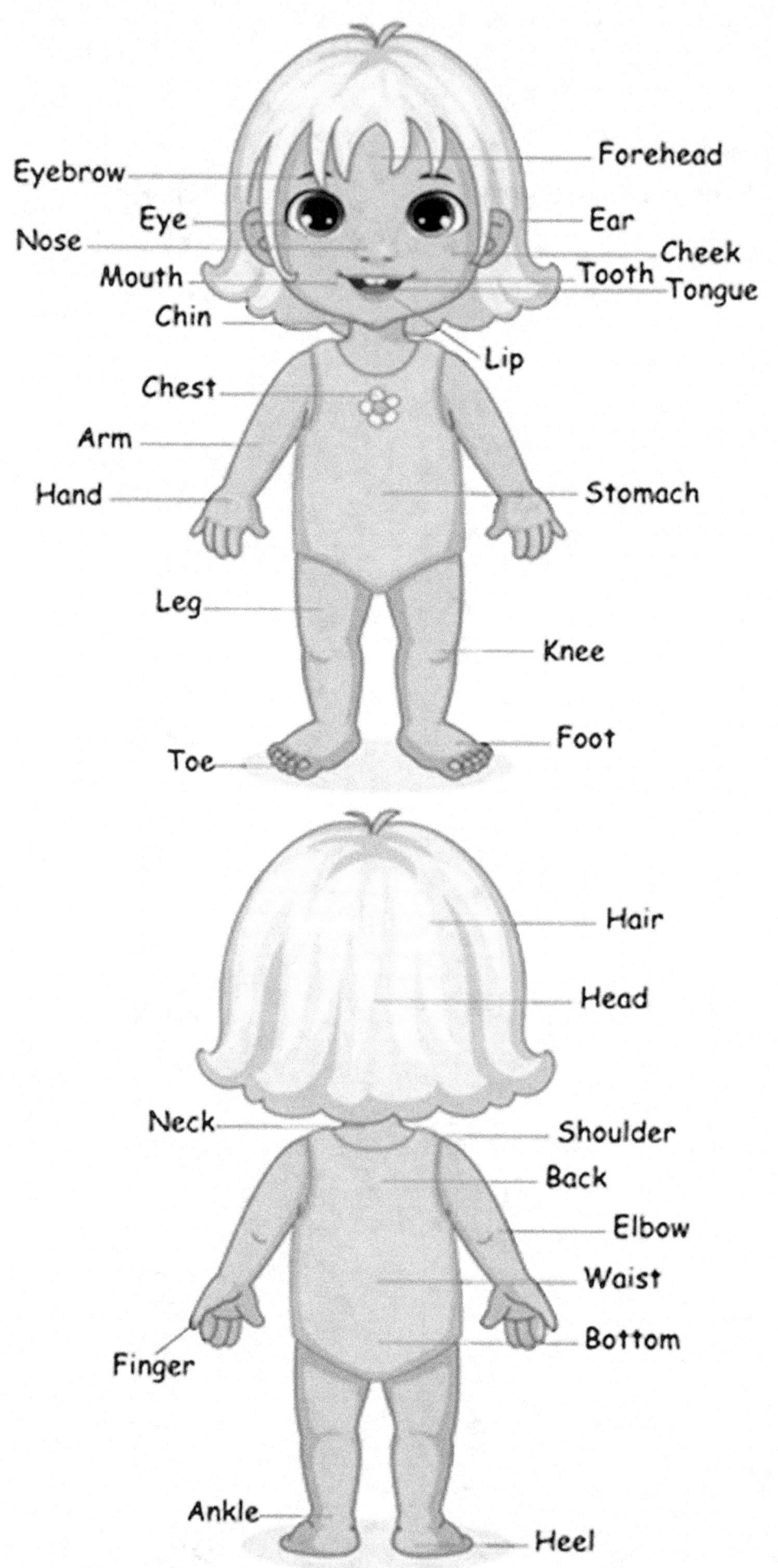

The five senses

5 SENSES

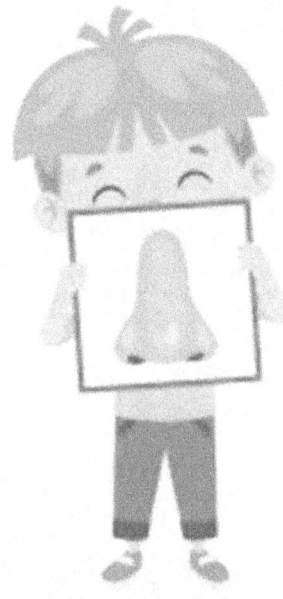

SMELL

TOUCH

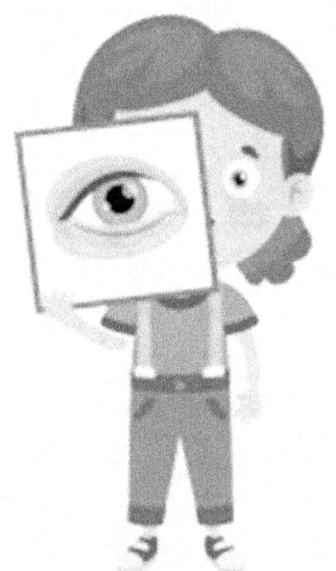

SIGHT

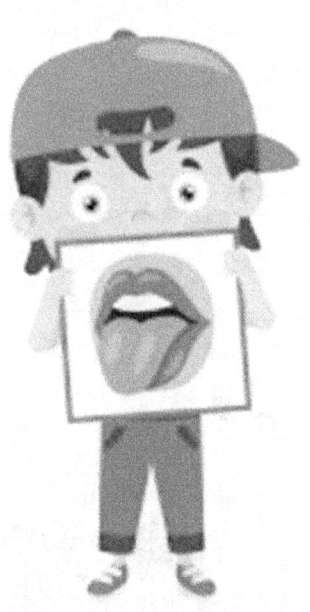

TASTE

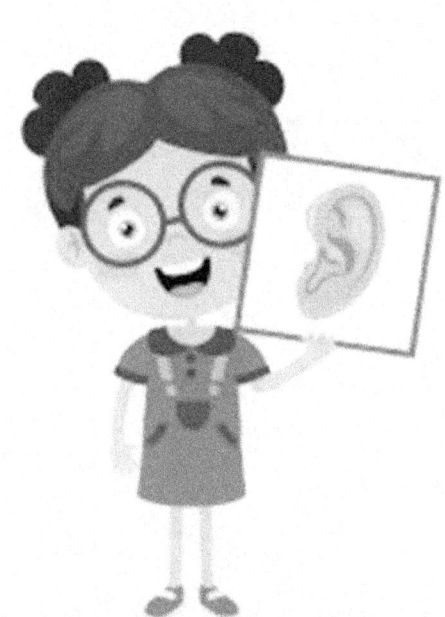

HEARING

MATCH THE PICTURES

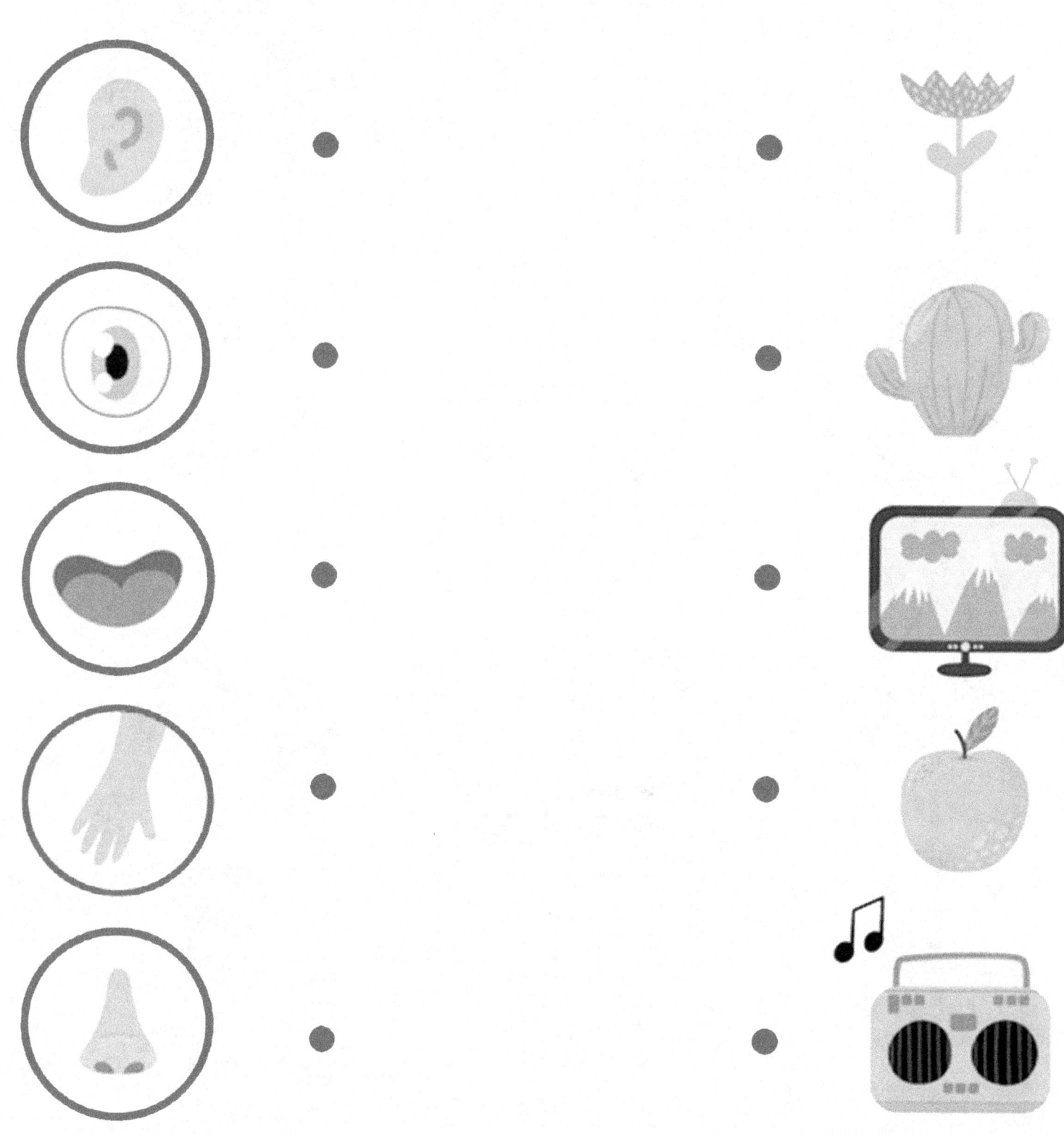

MATCH THE PICTURES

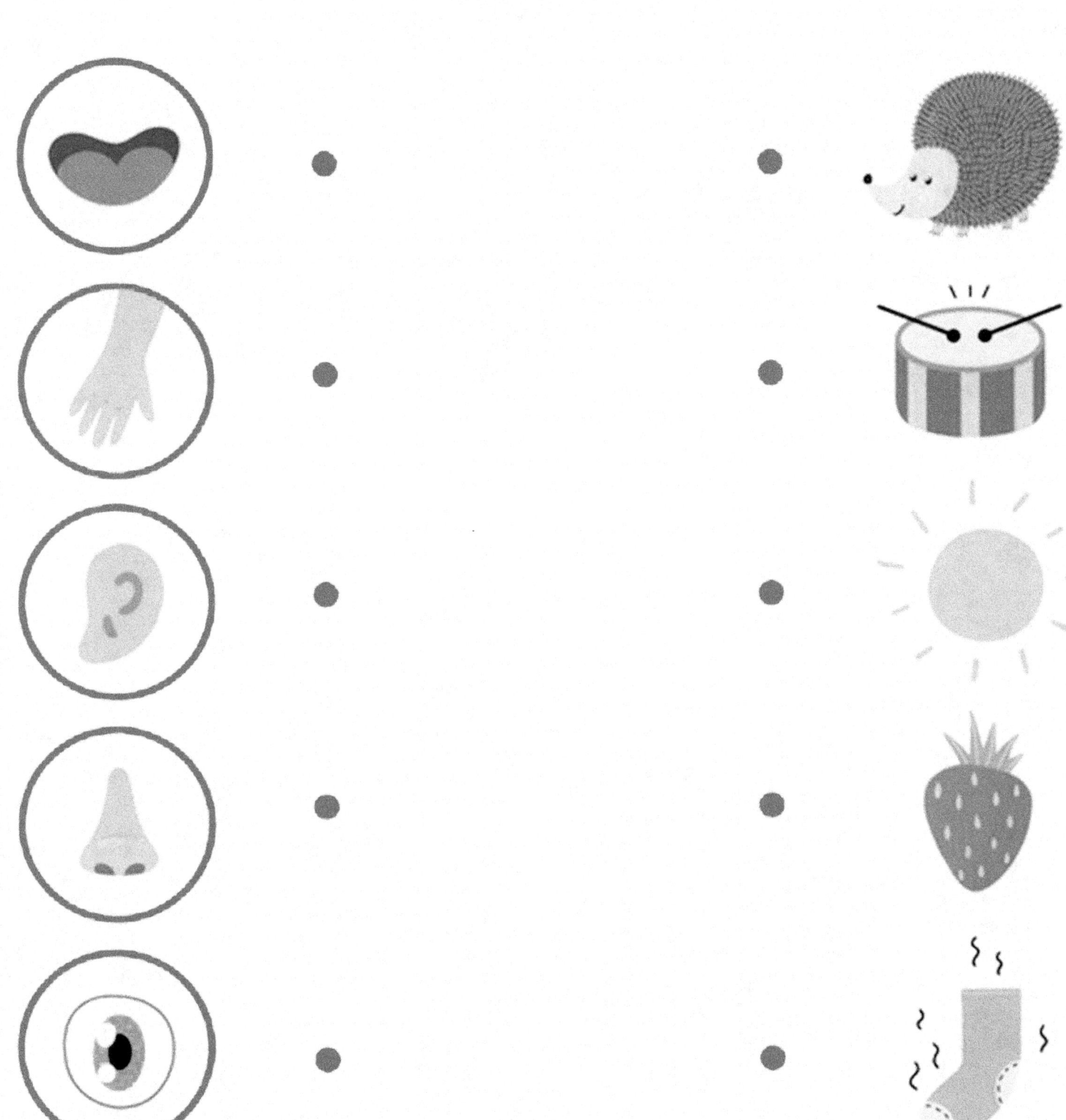

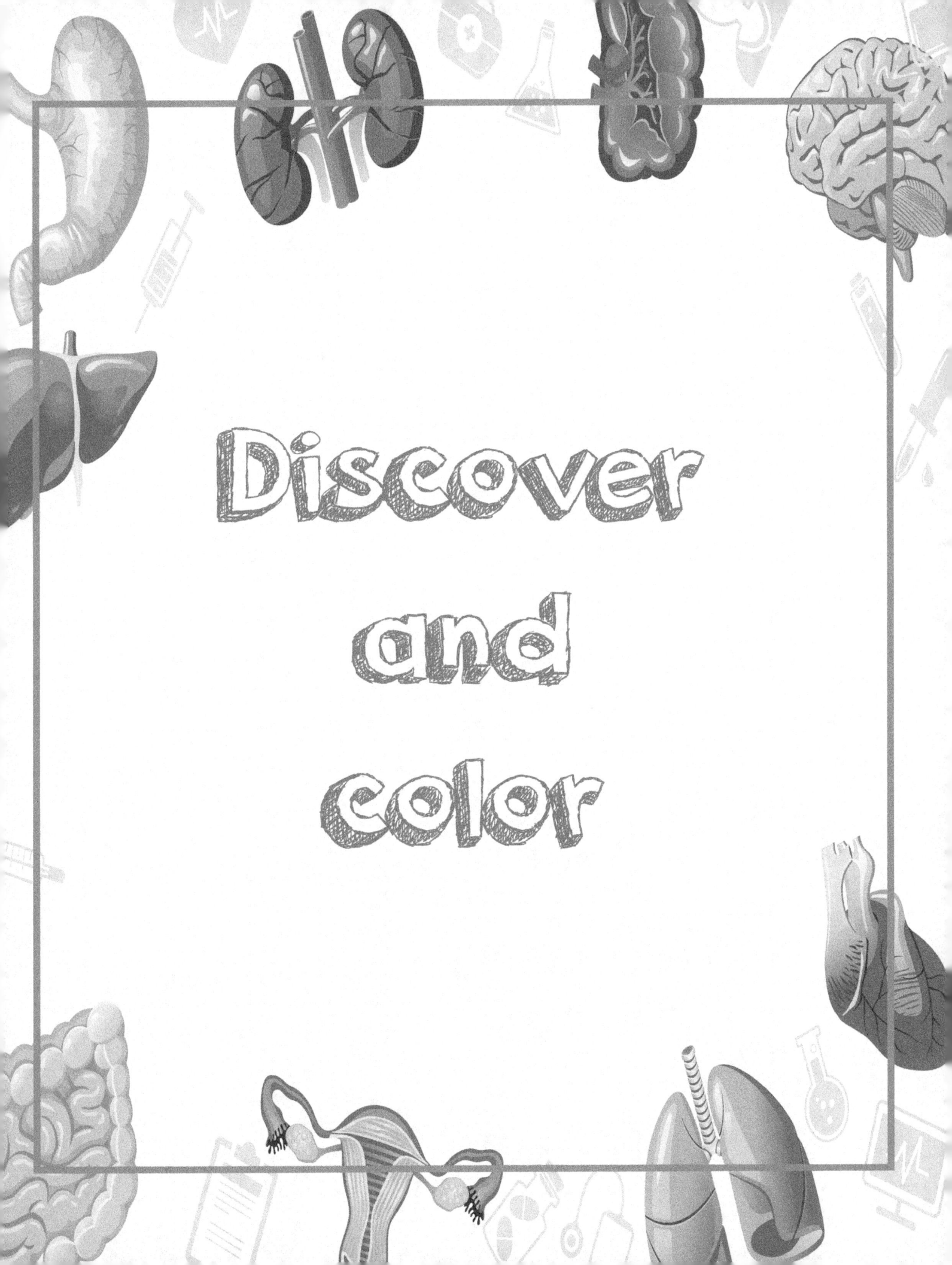

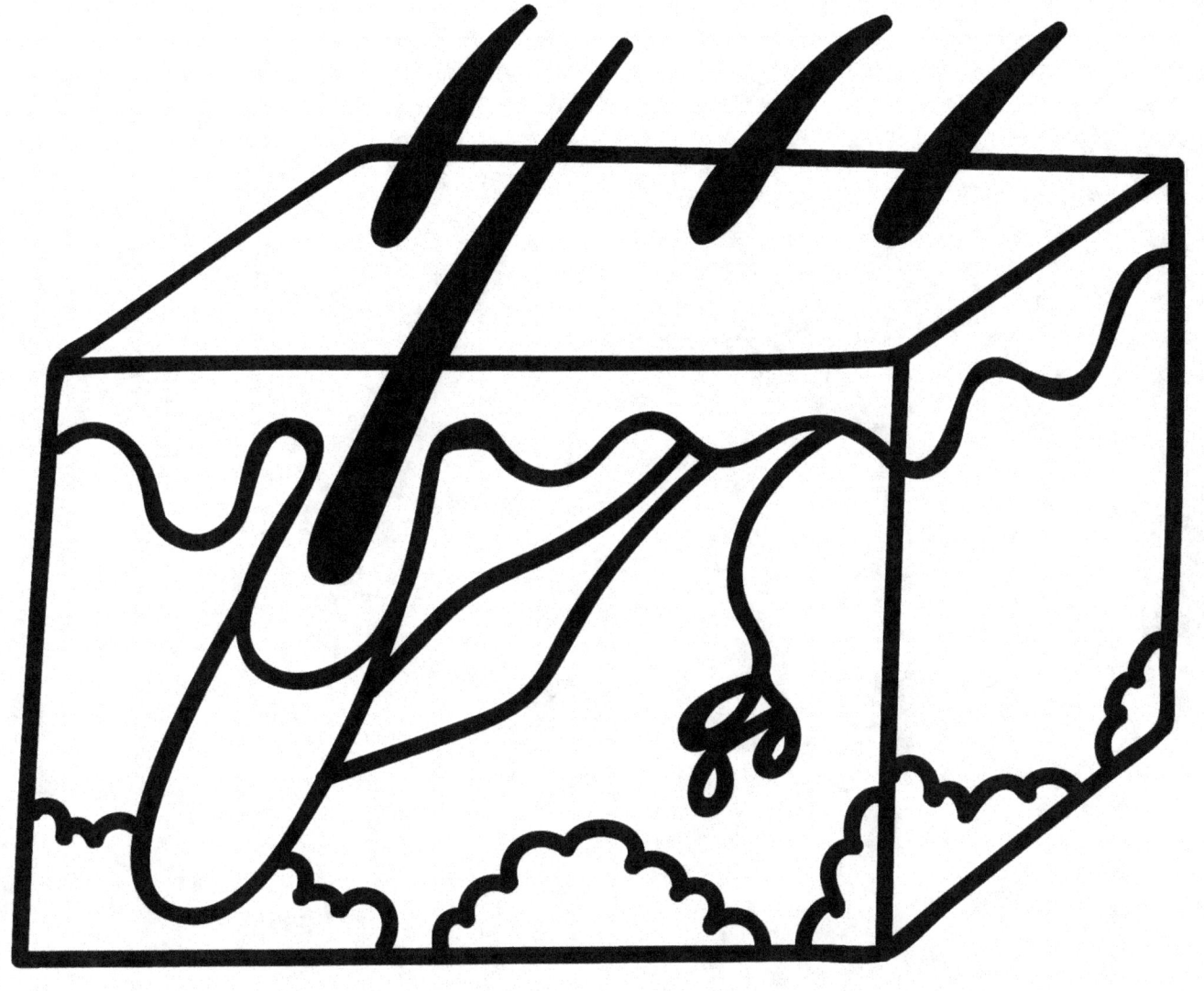

SKIN

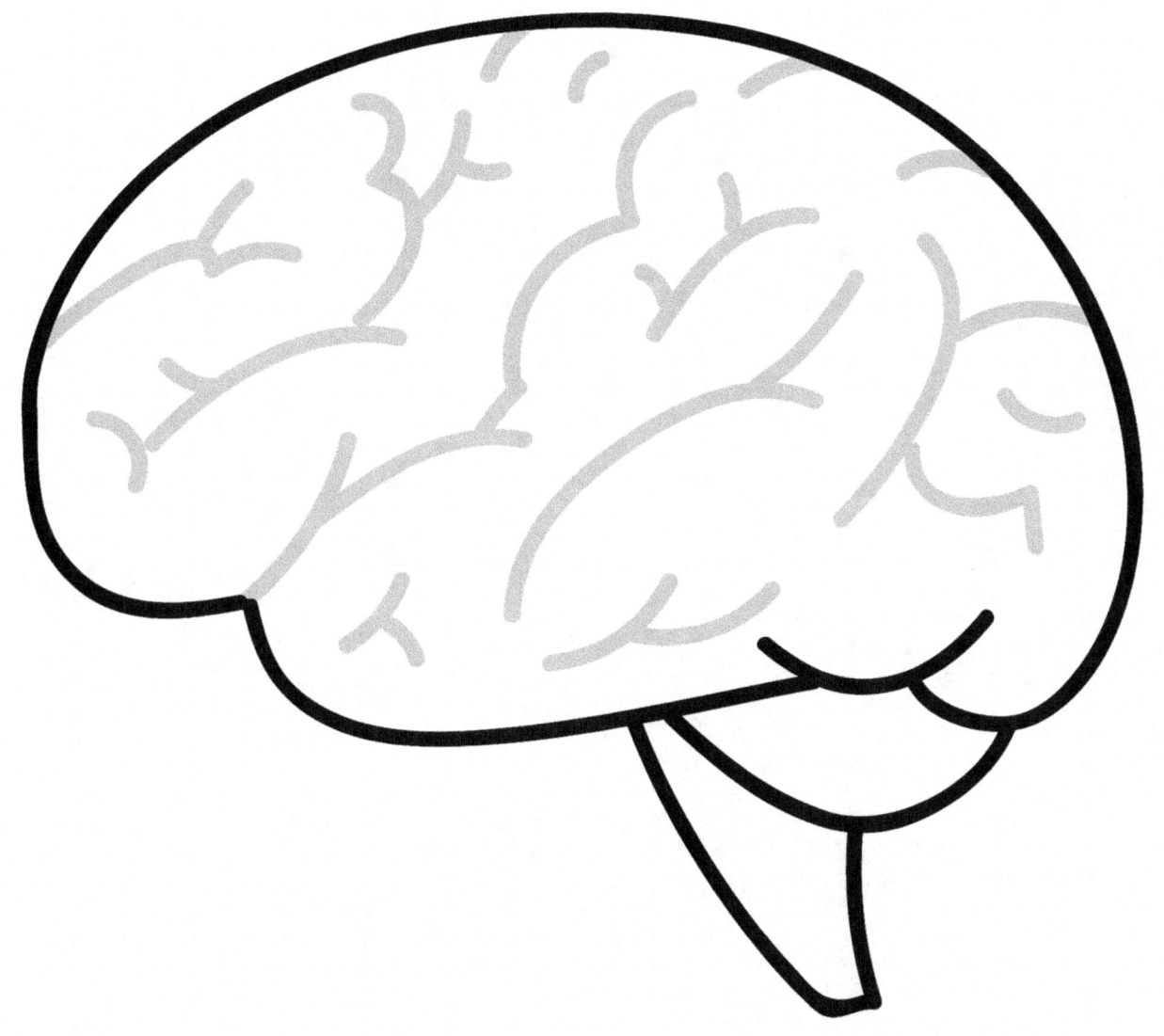

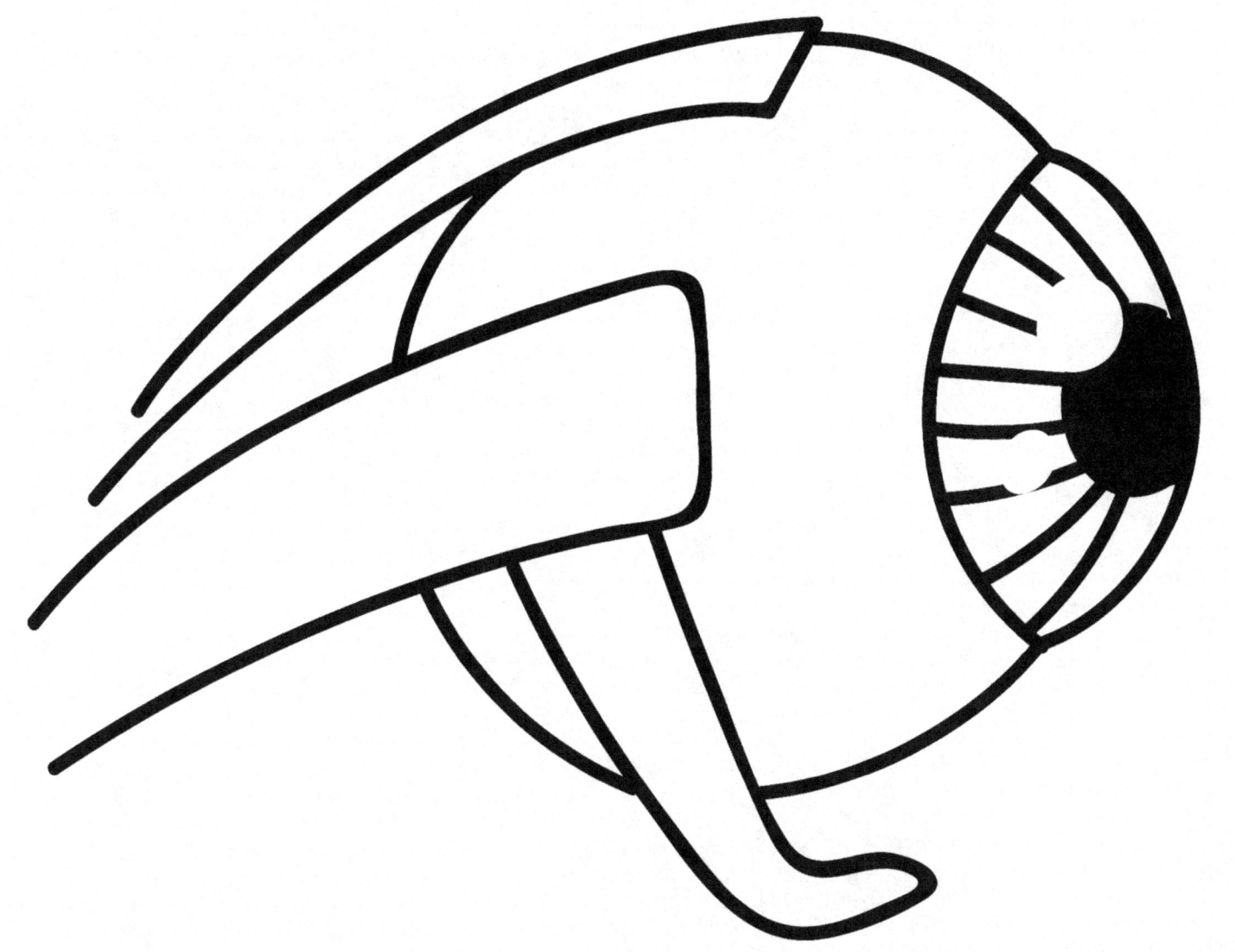
EYE BALL

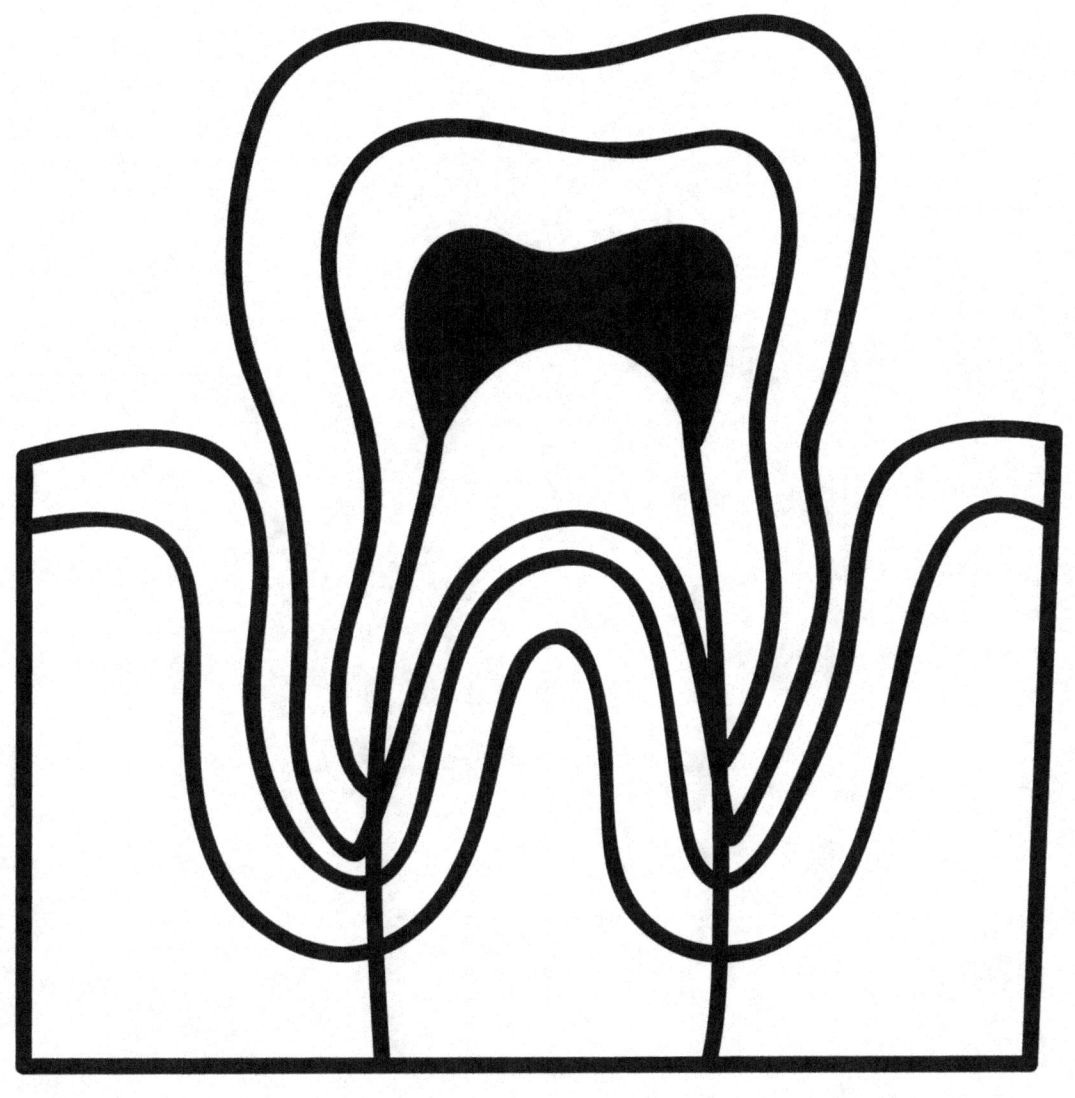

TOOTH

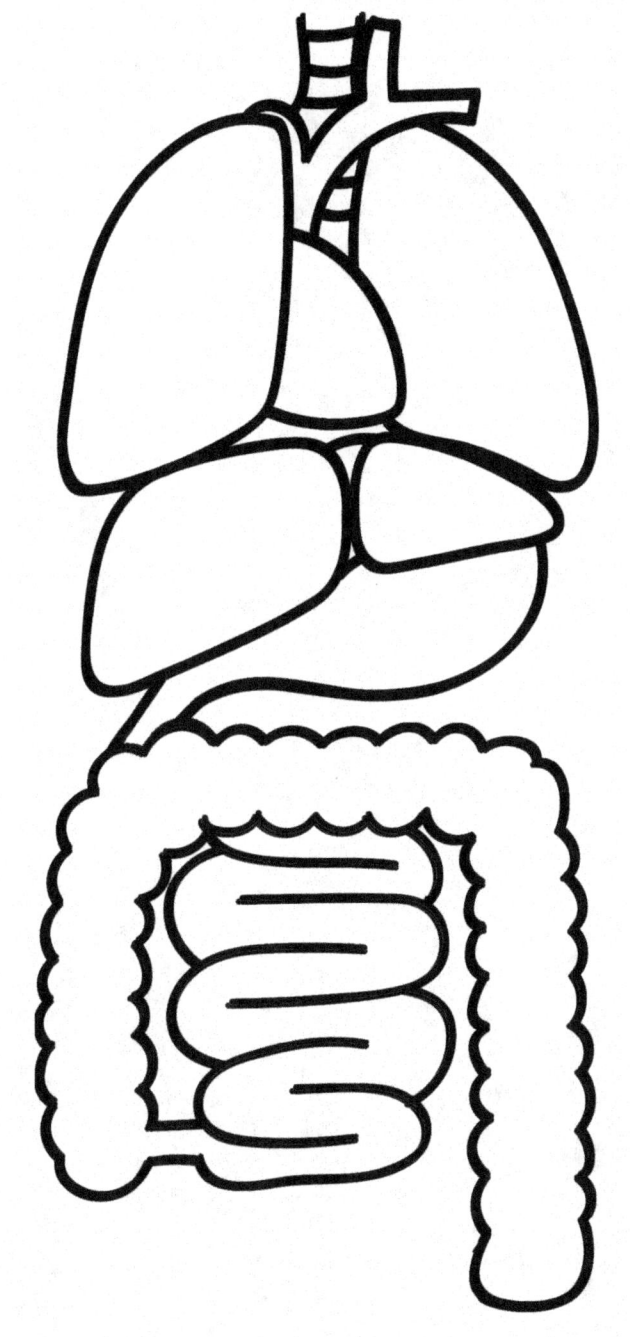

ORGANS

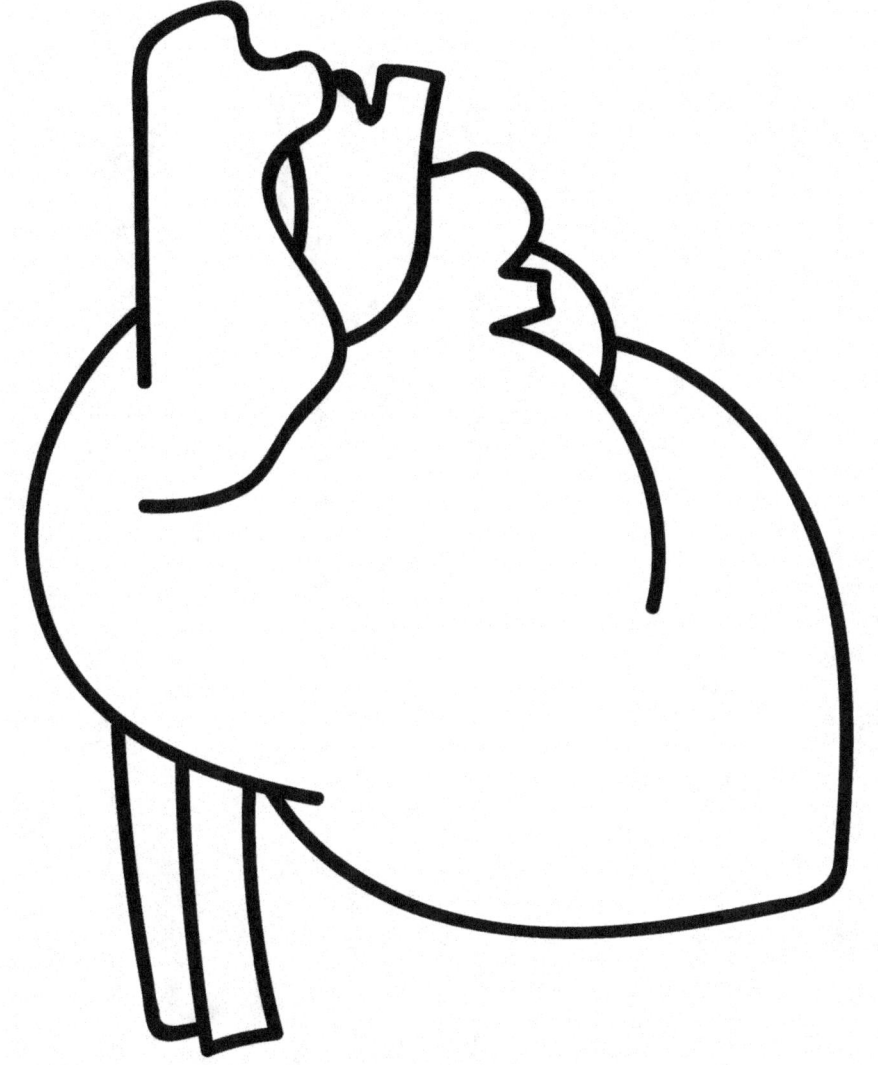

HEART

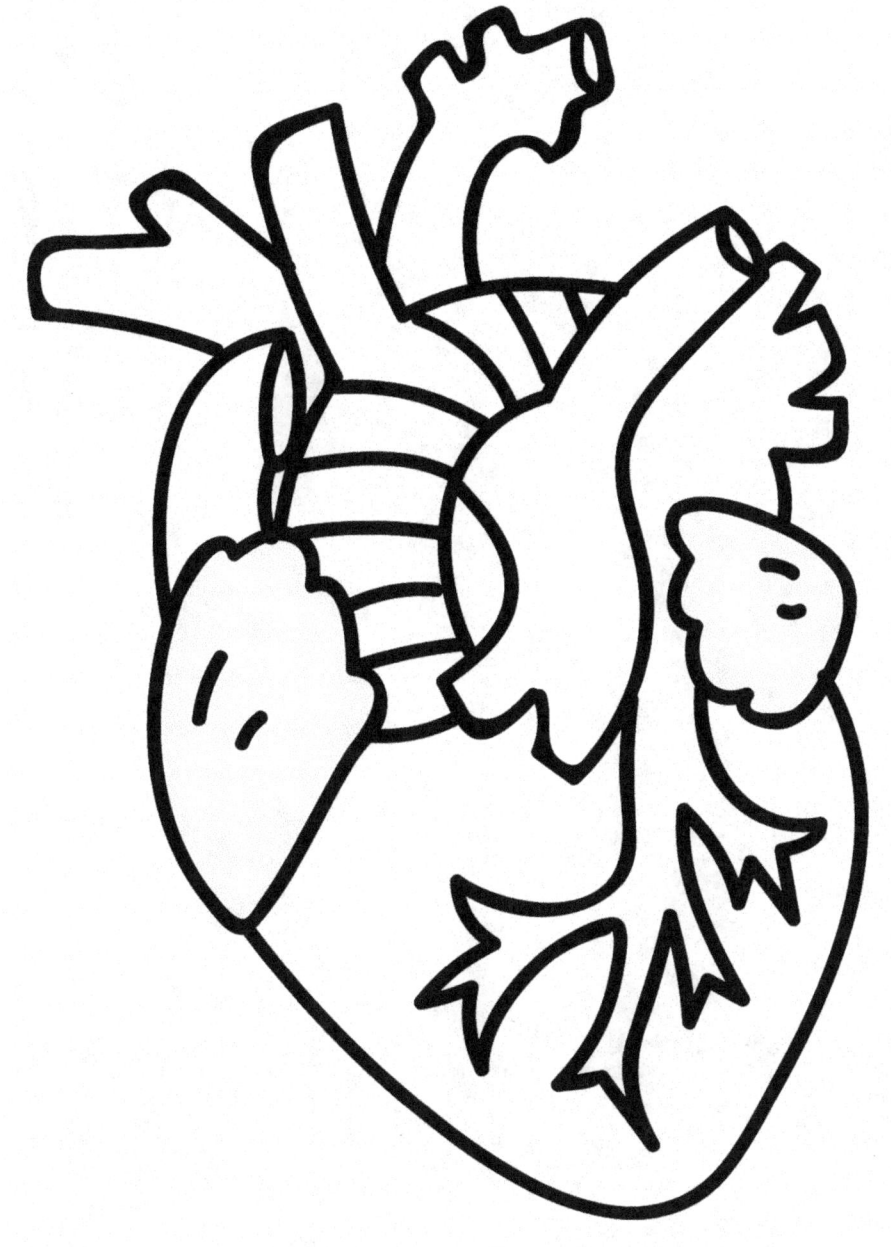

HEART

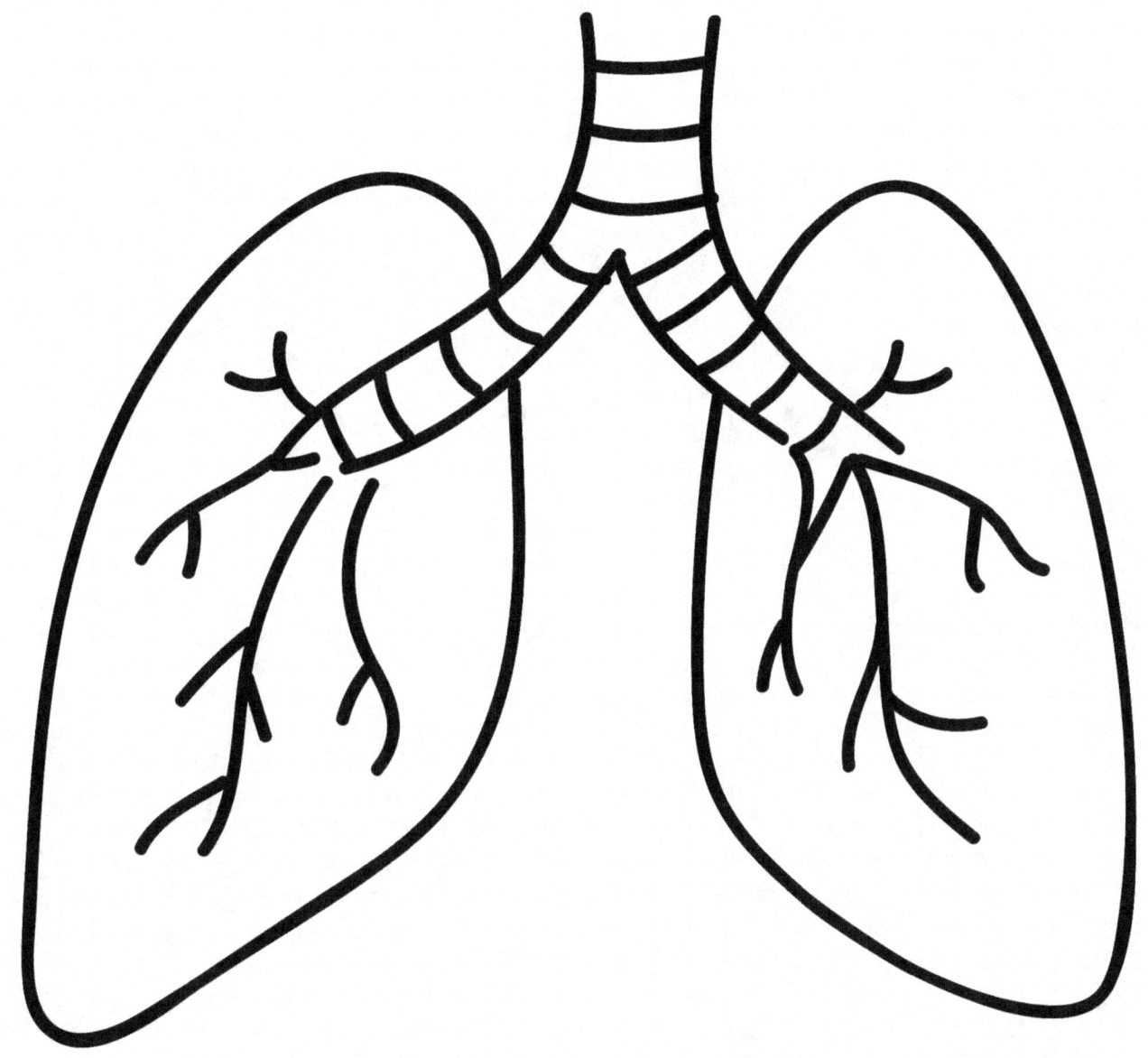

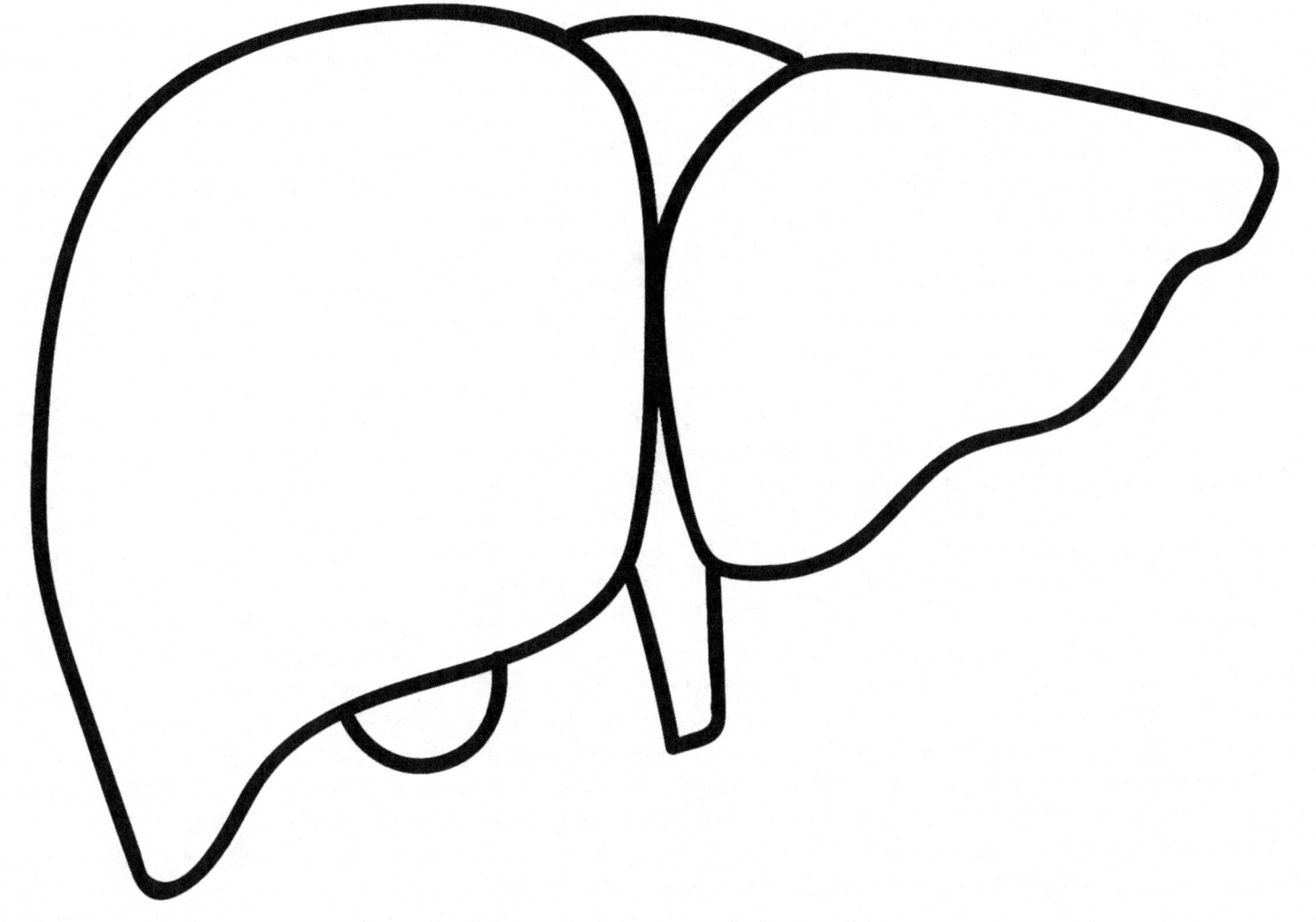

LIVER

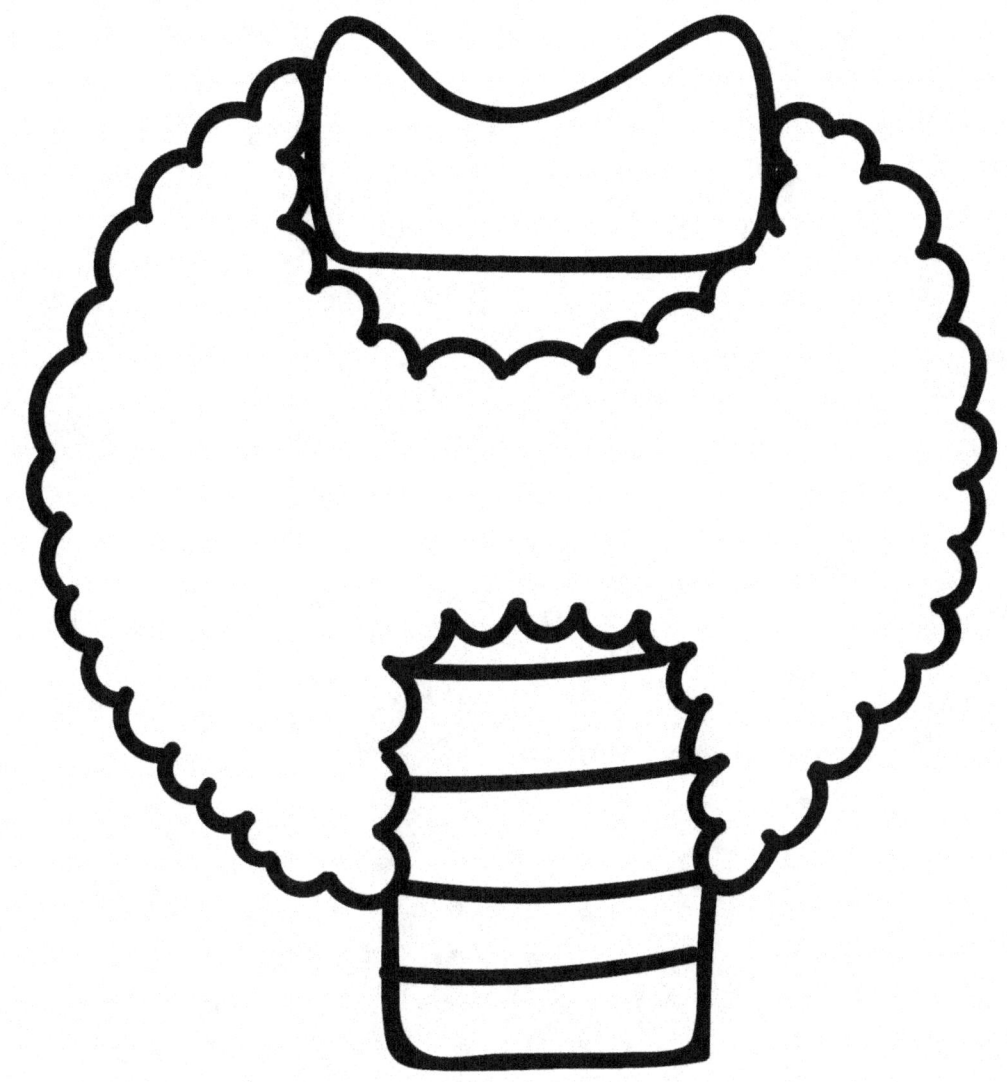

THYROID

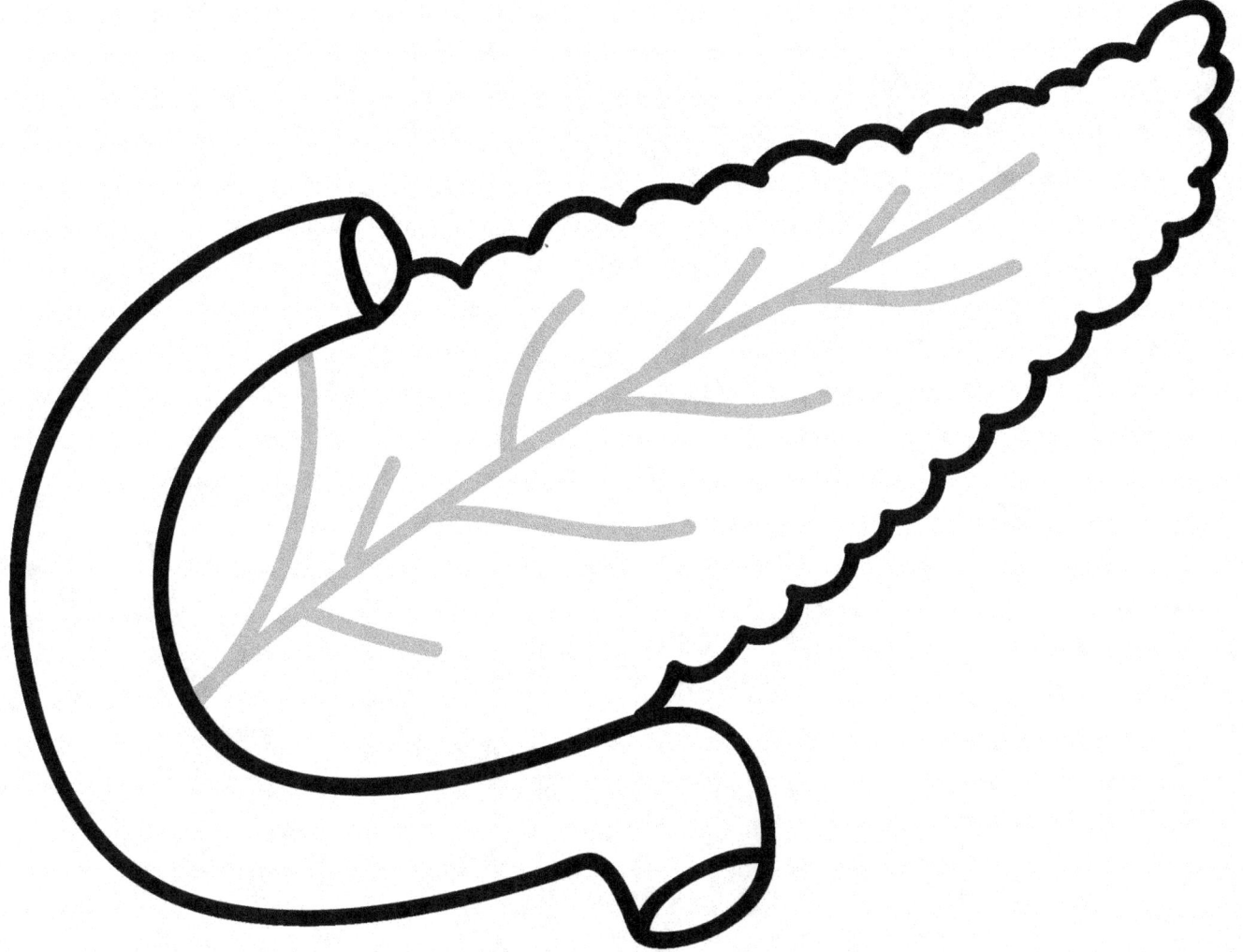

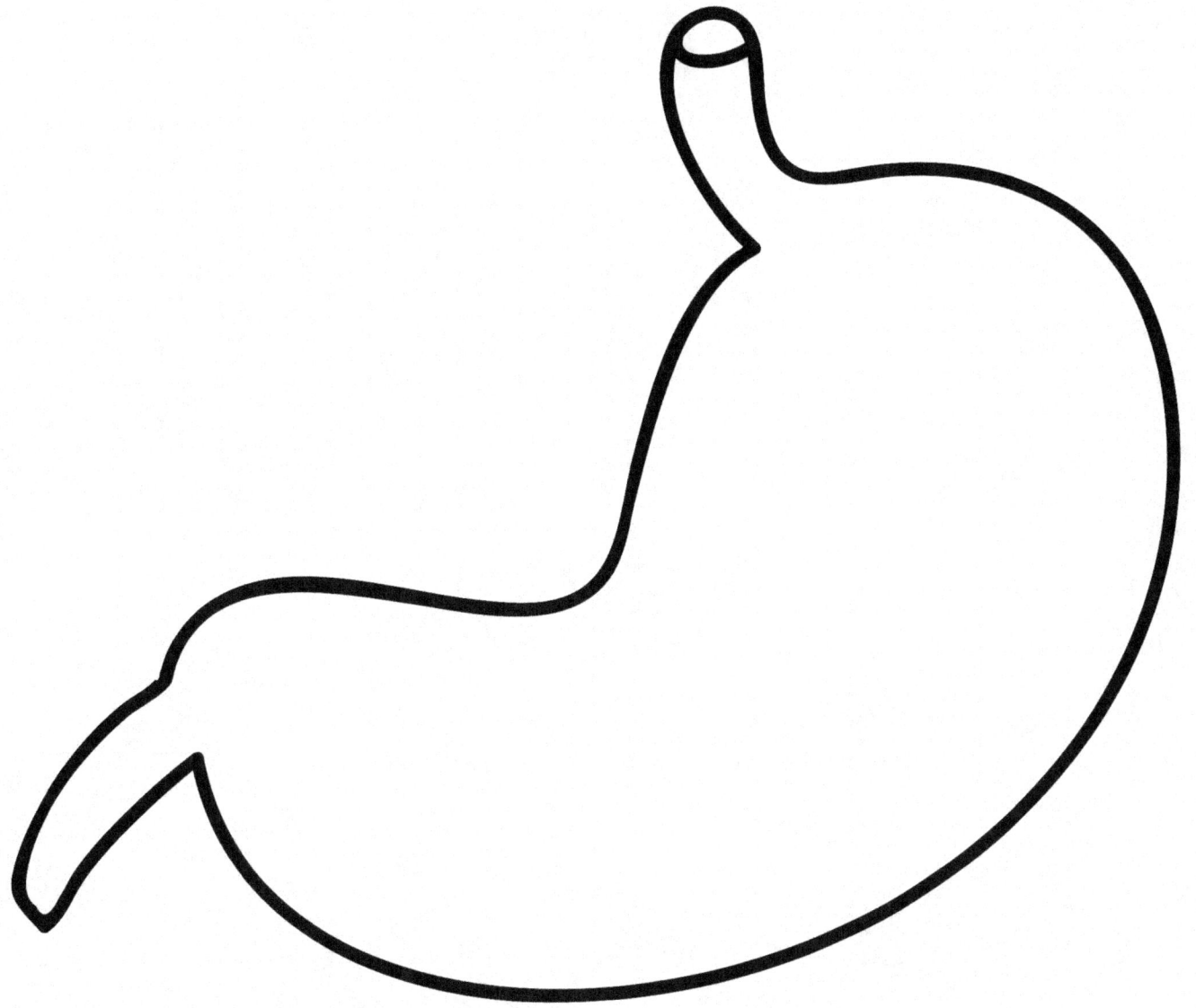

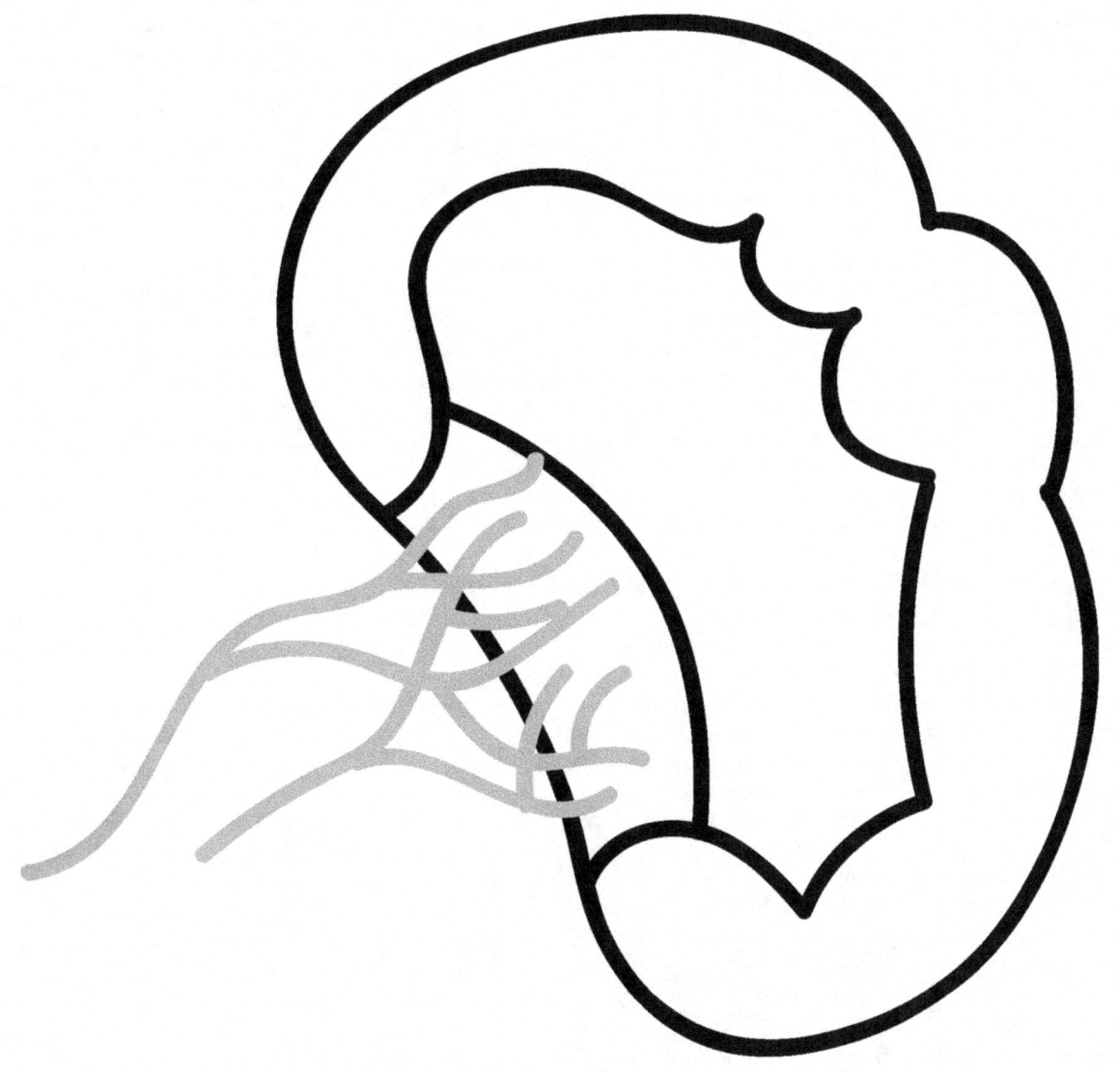

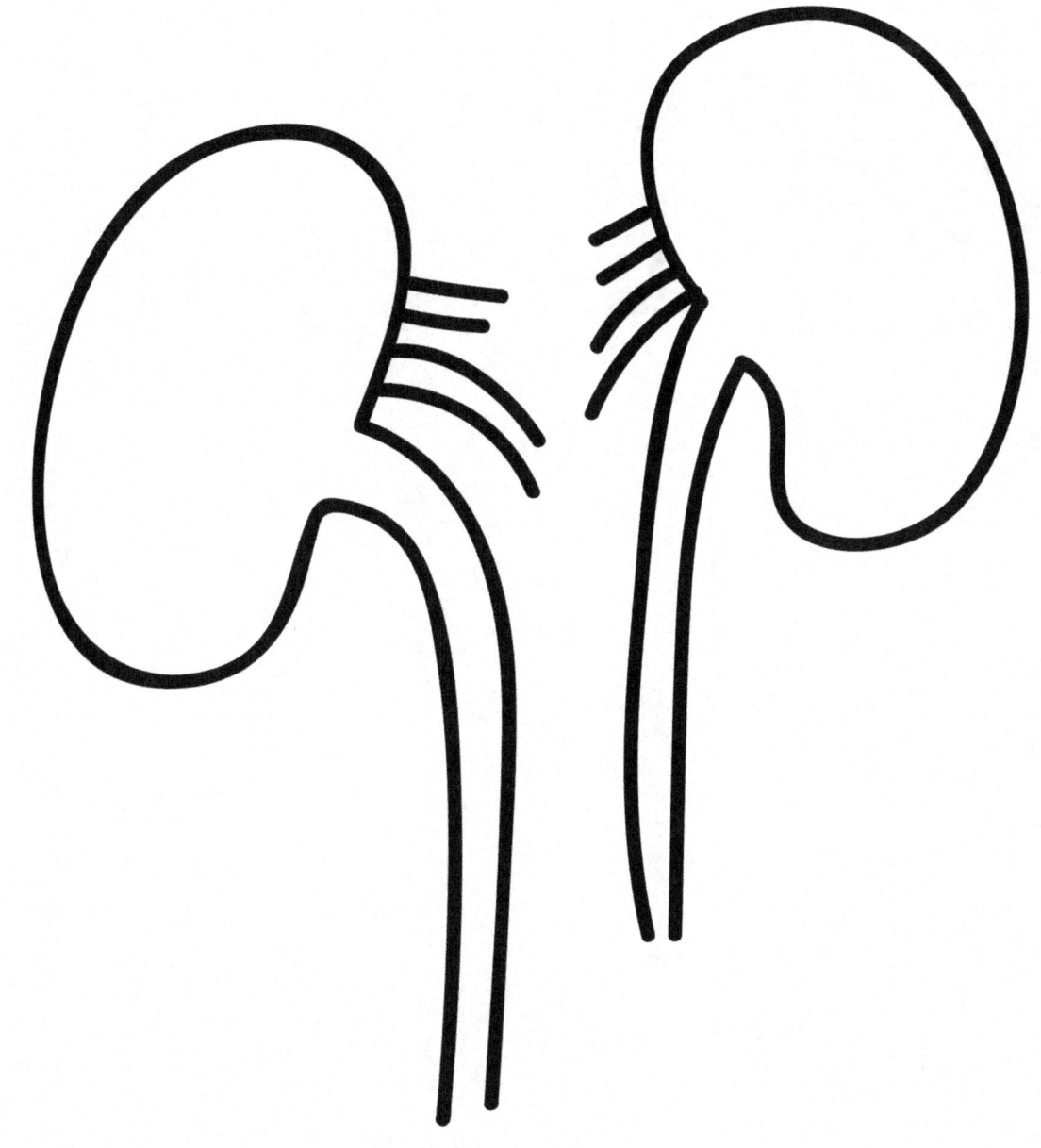

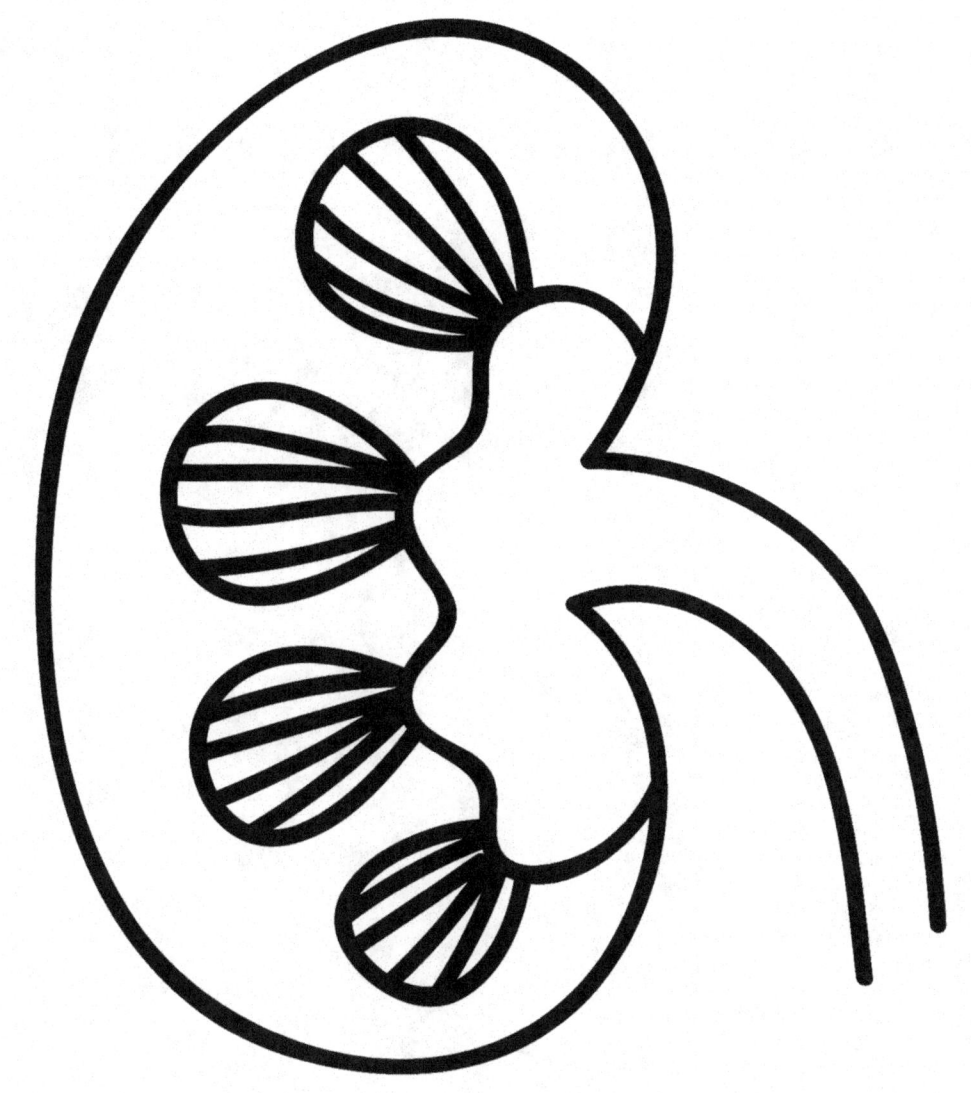

KIDNEY

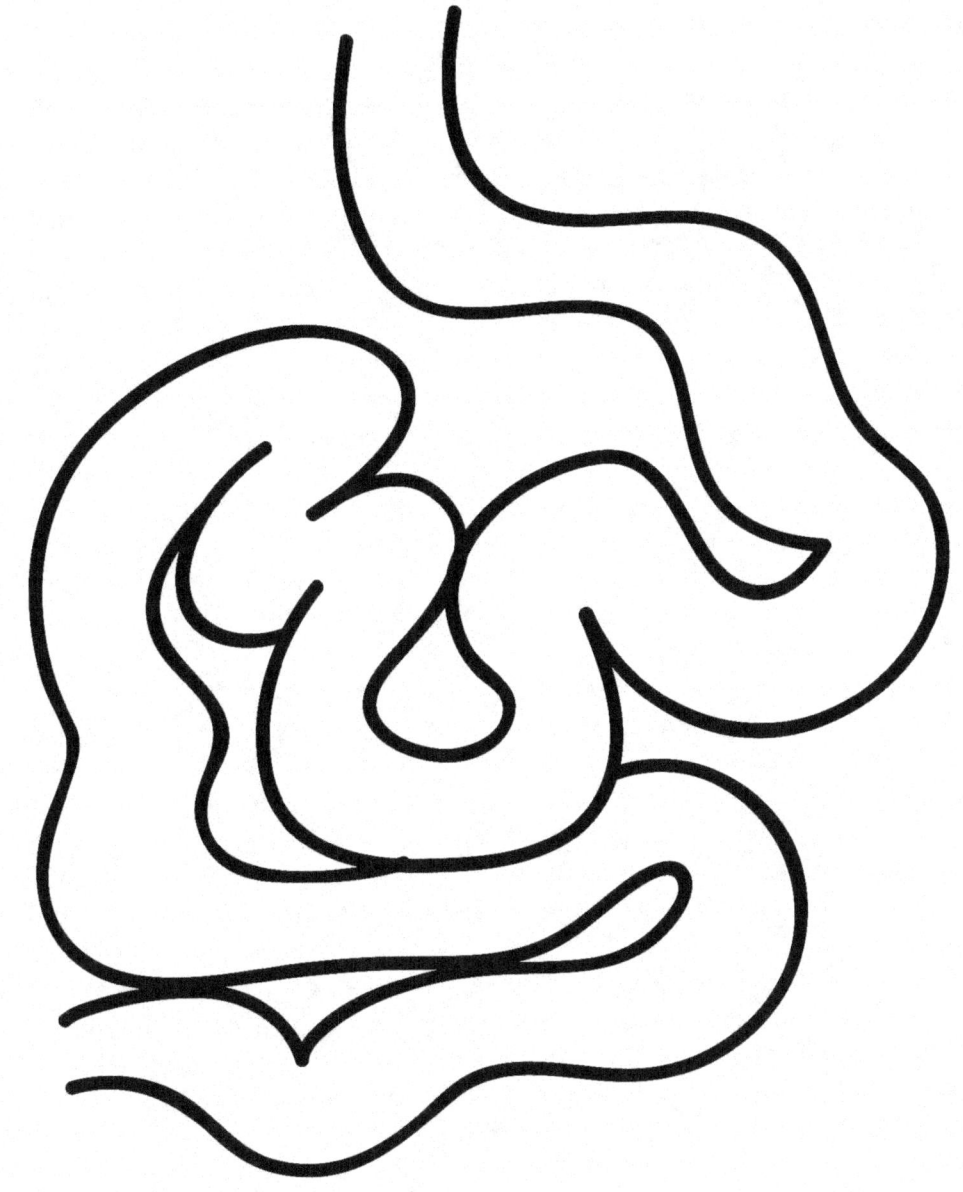

SMALL INTESTINE

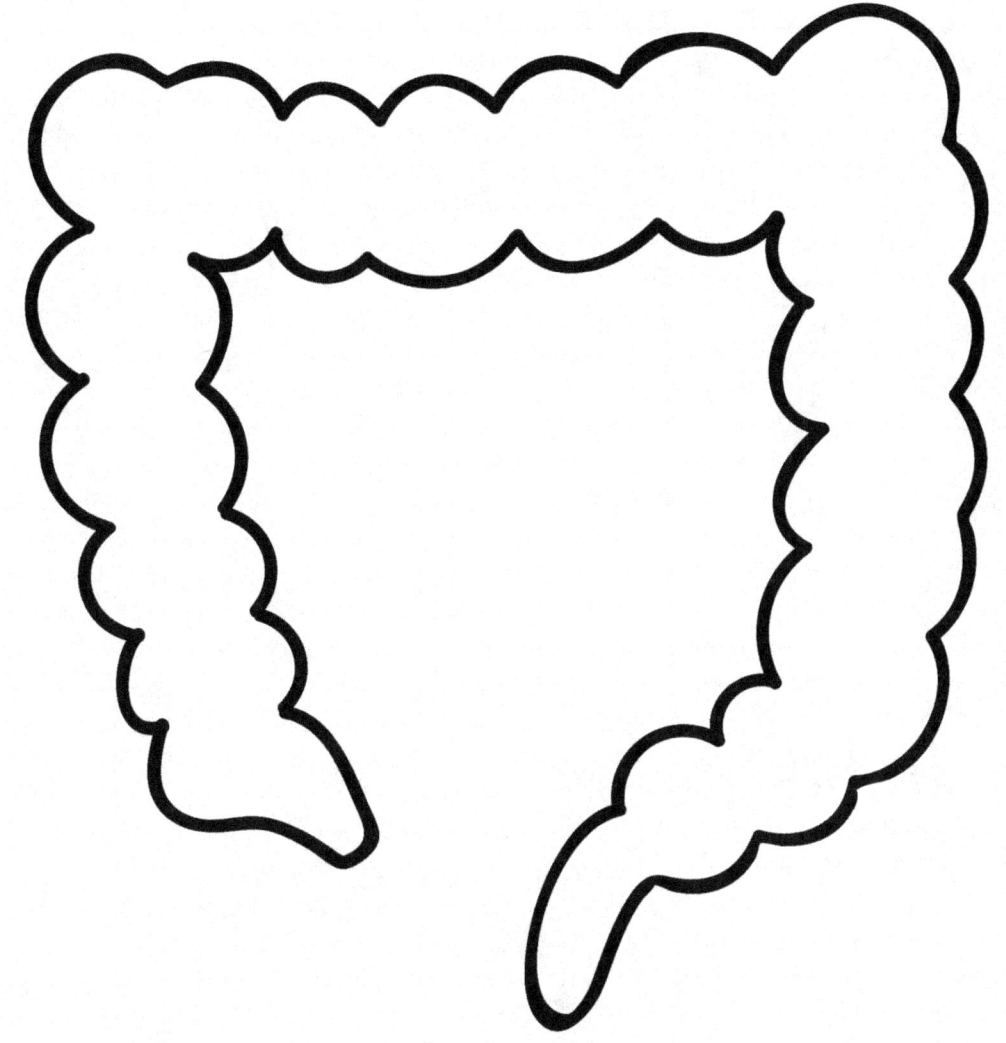

COLON

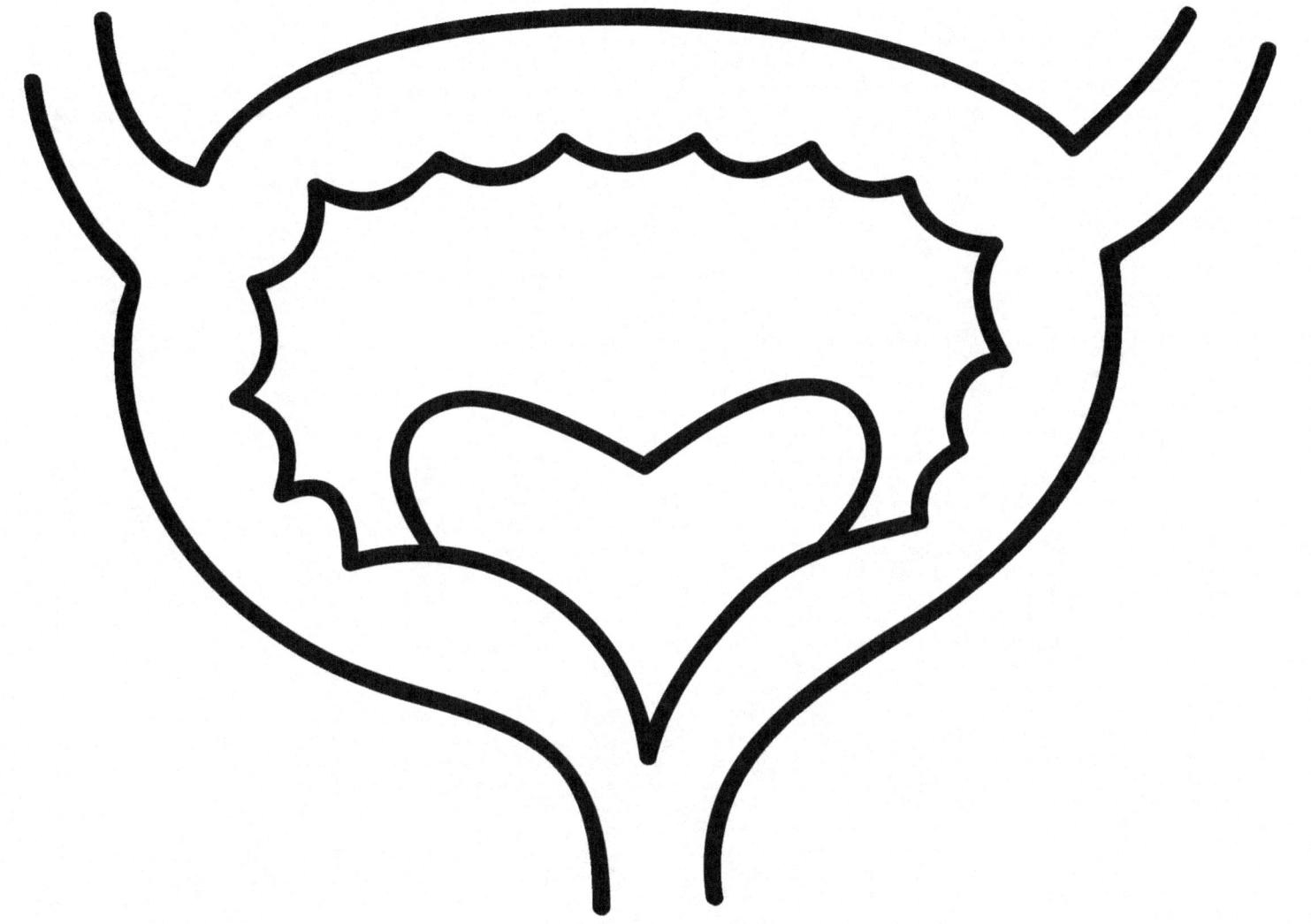

BLADDER

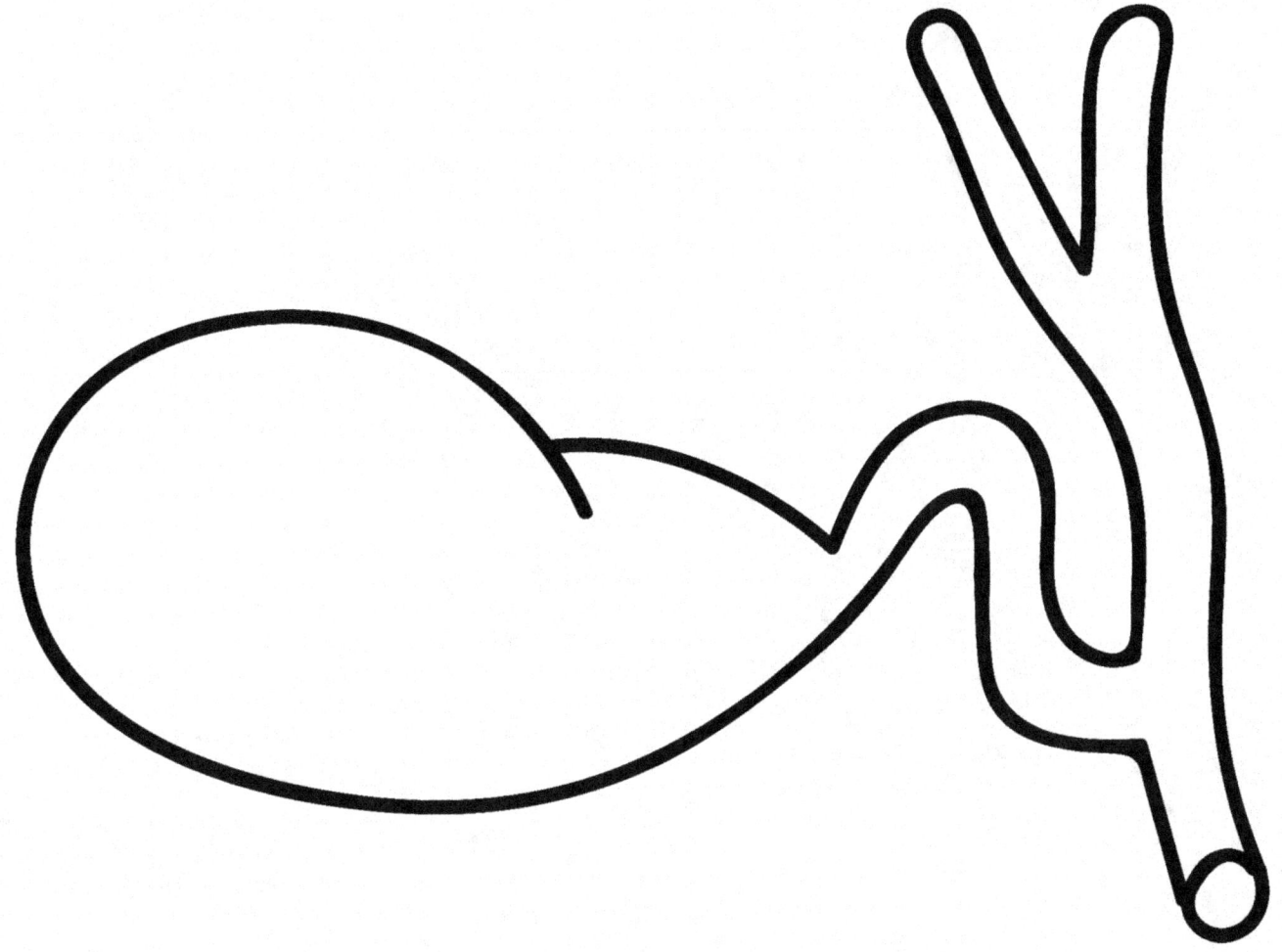

GALLBLADDER

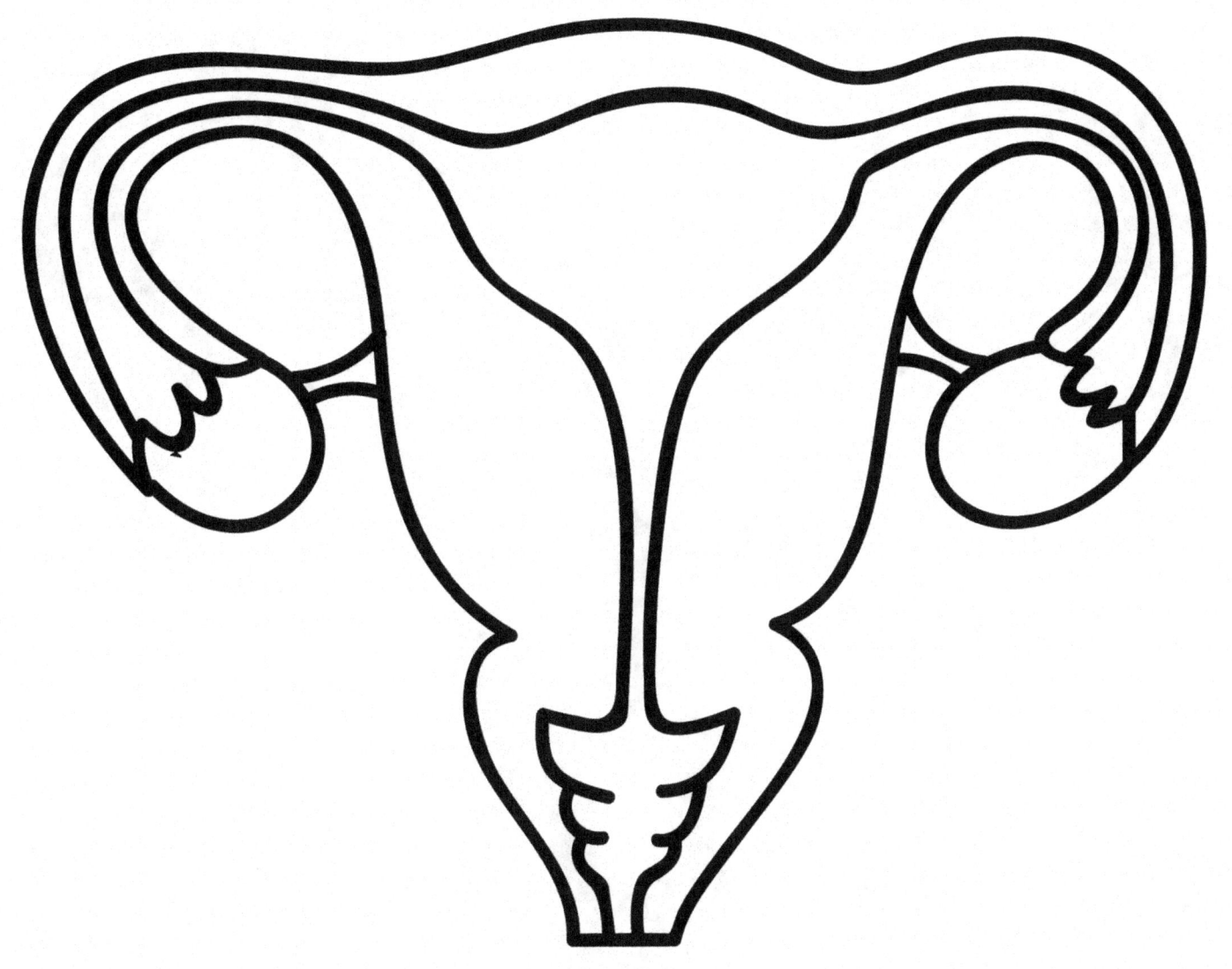

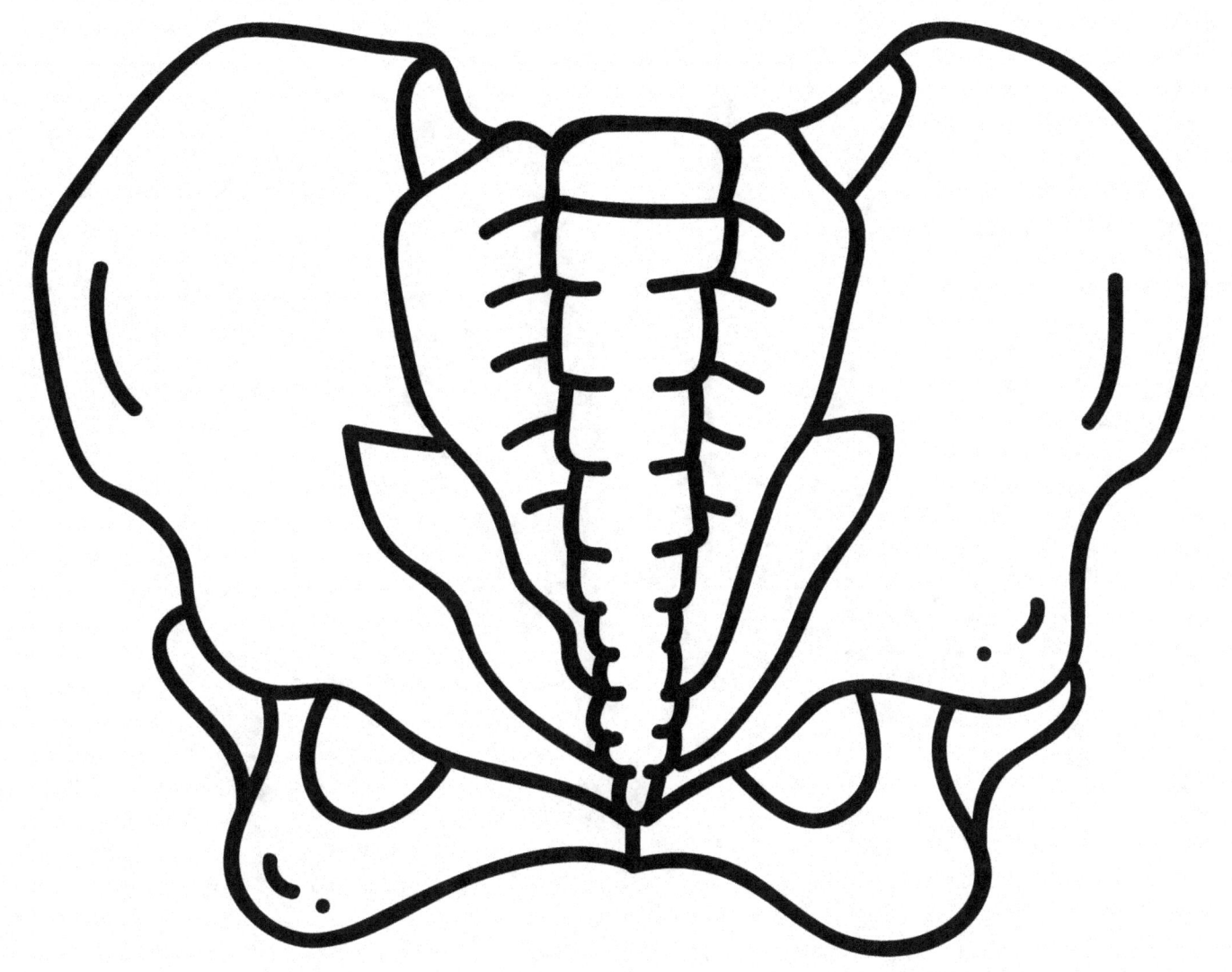

PELVIS

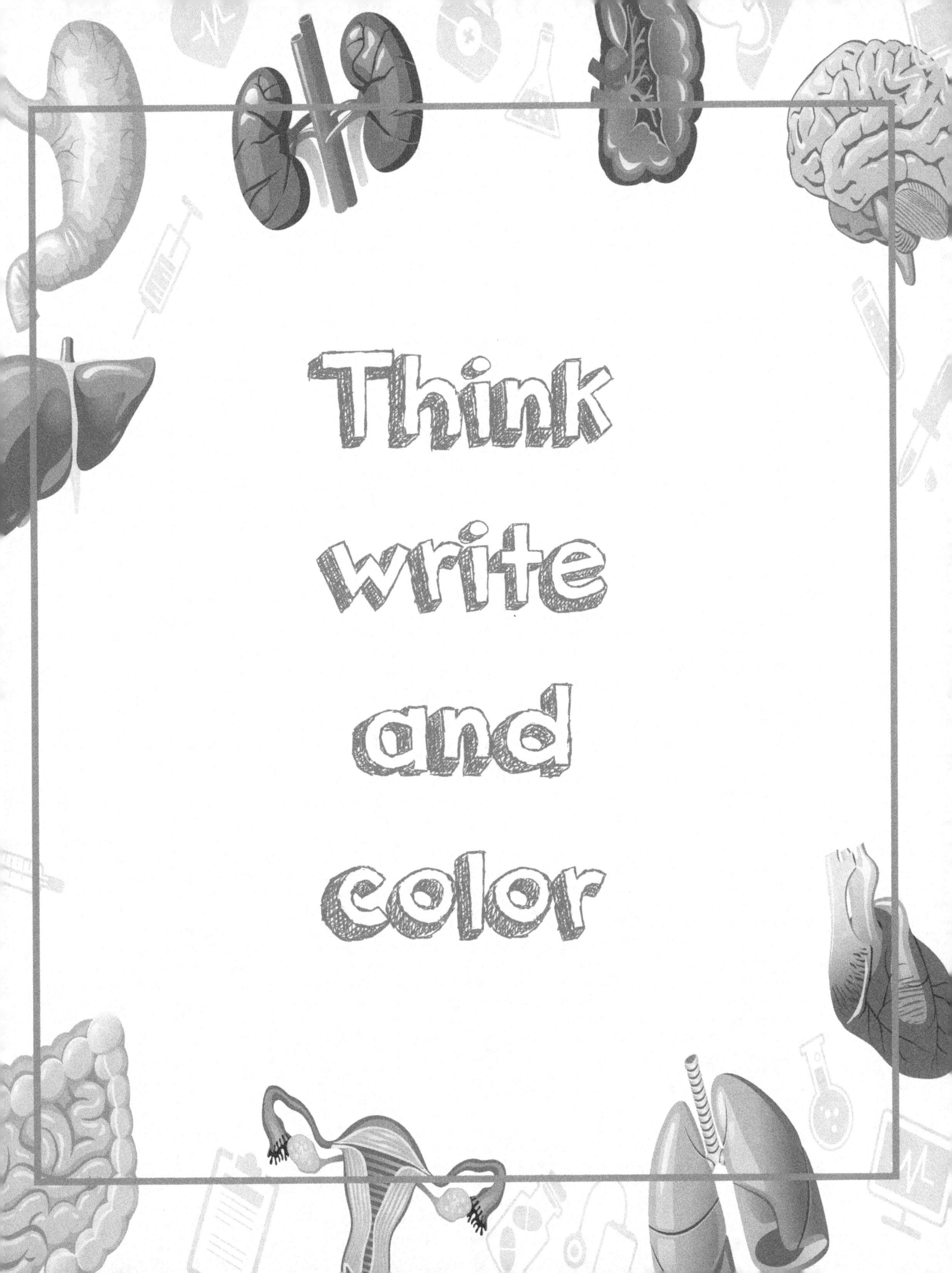

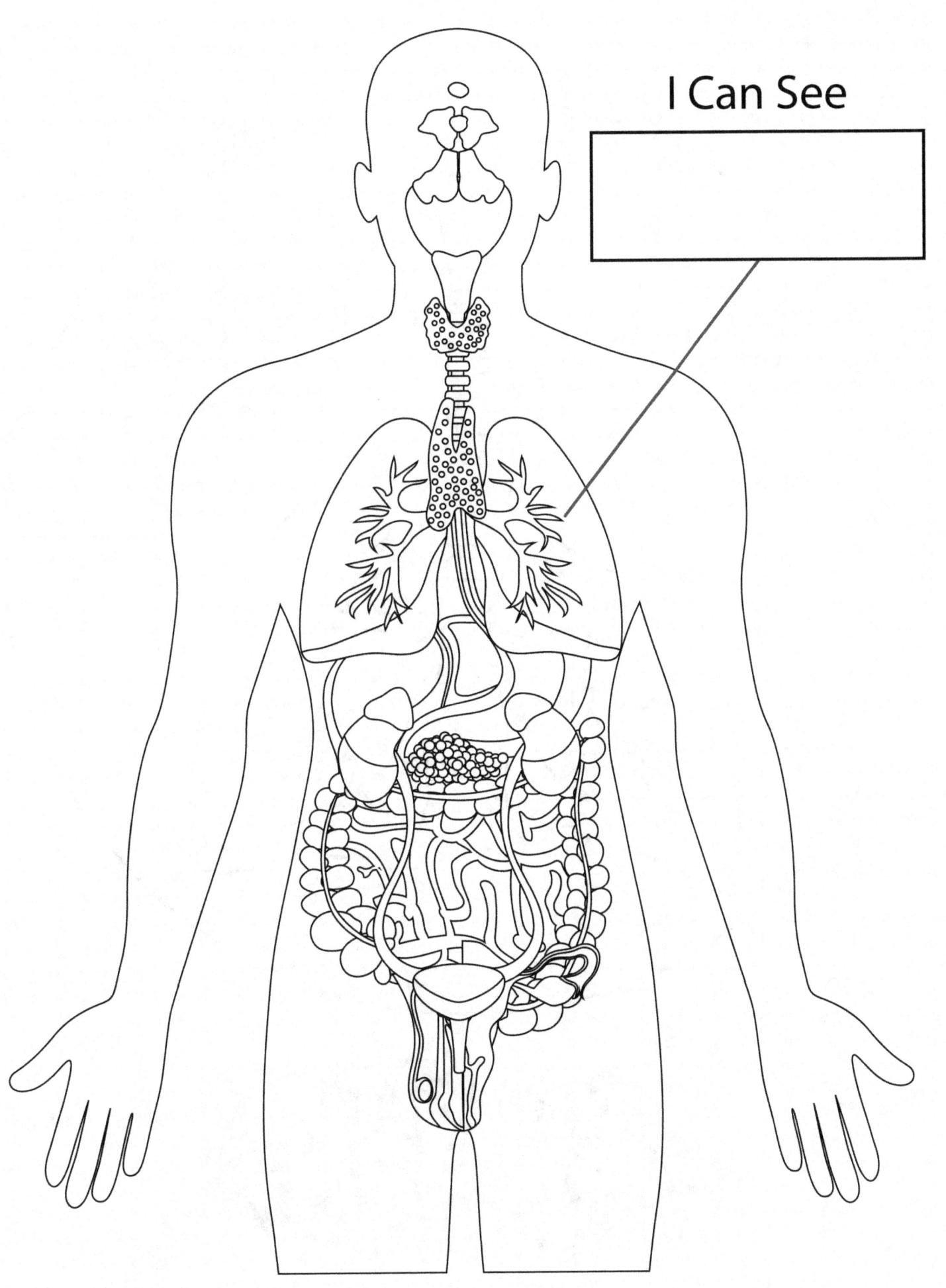

I Can See

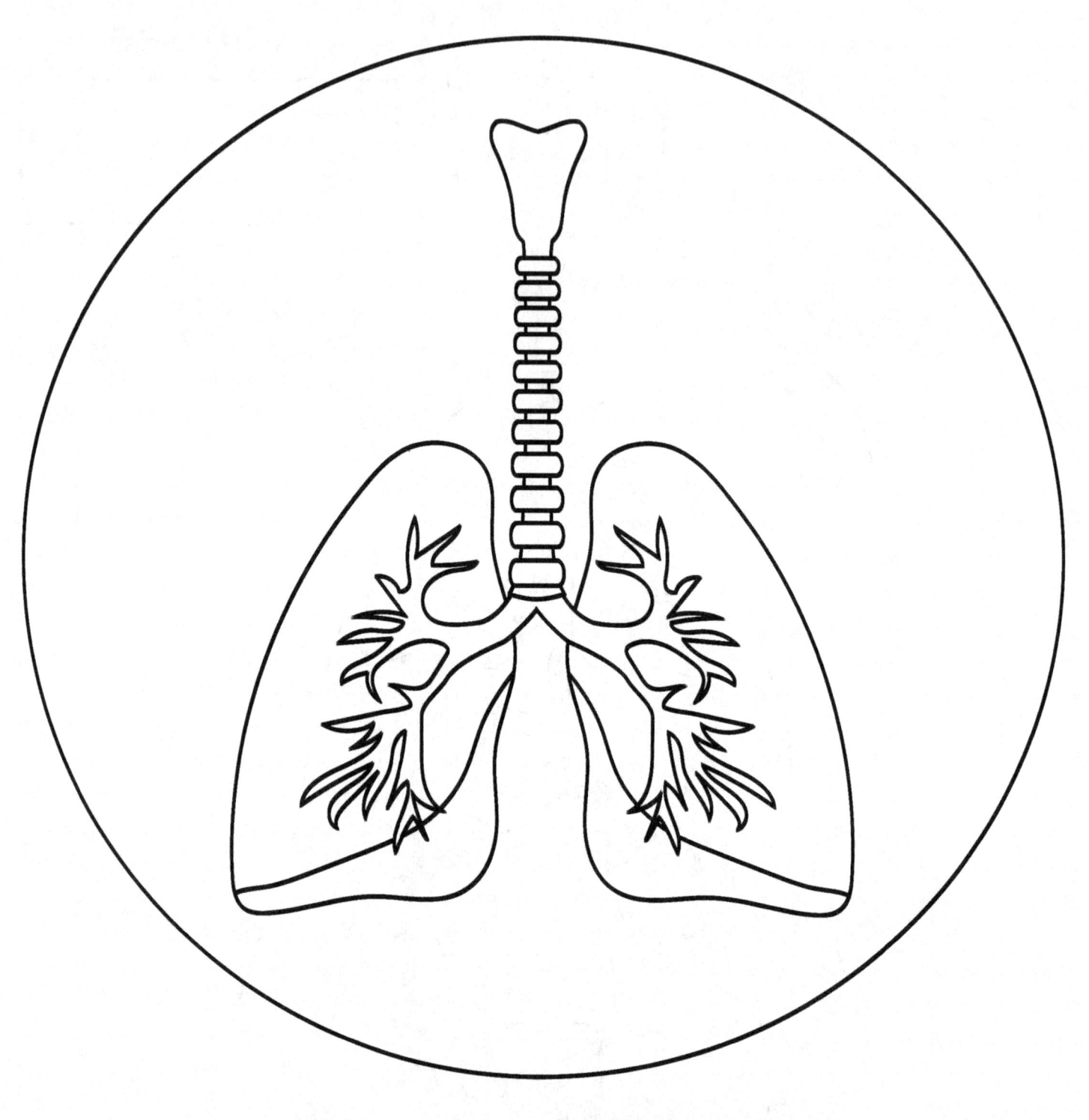

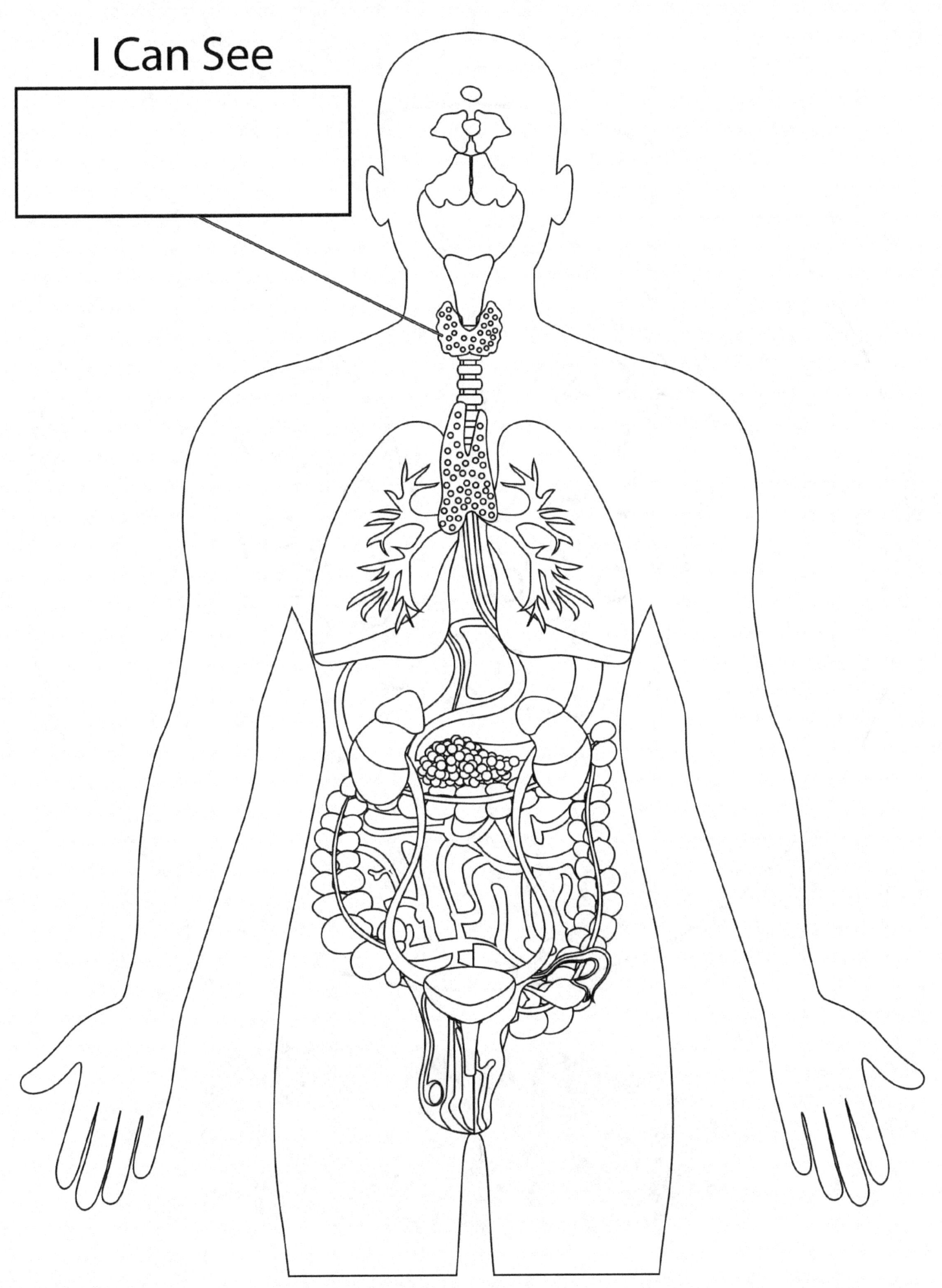

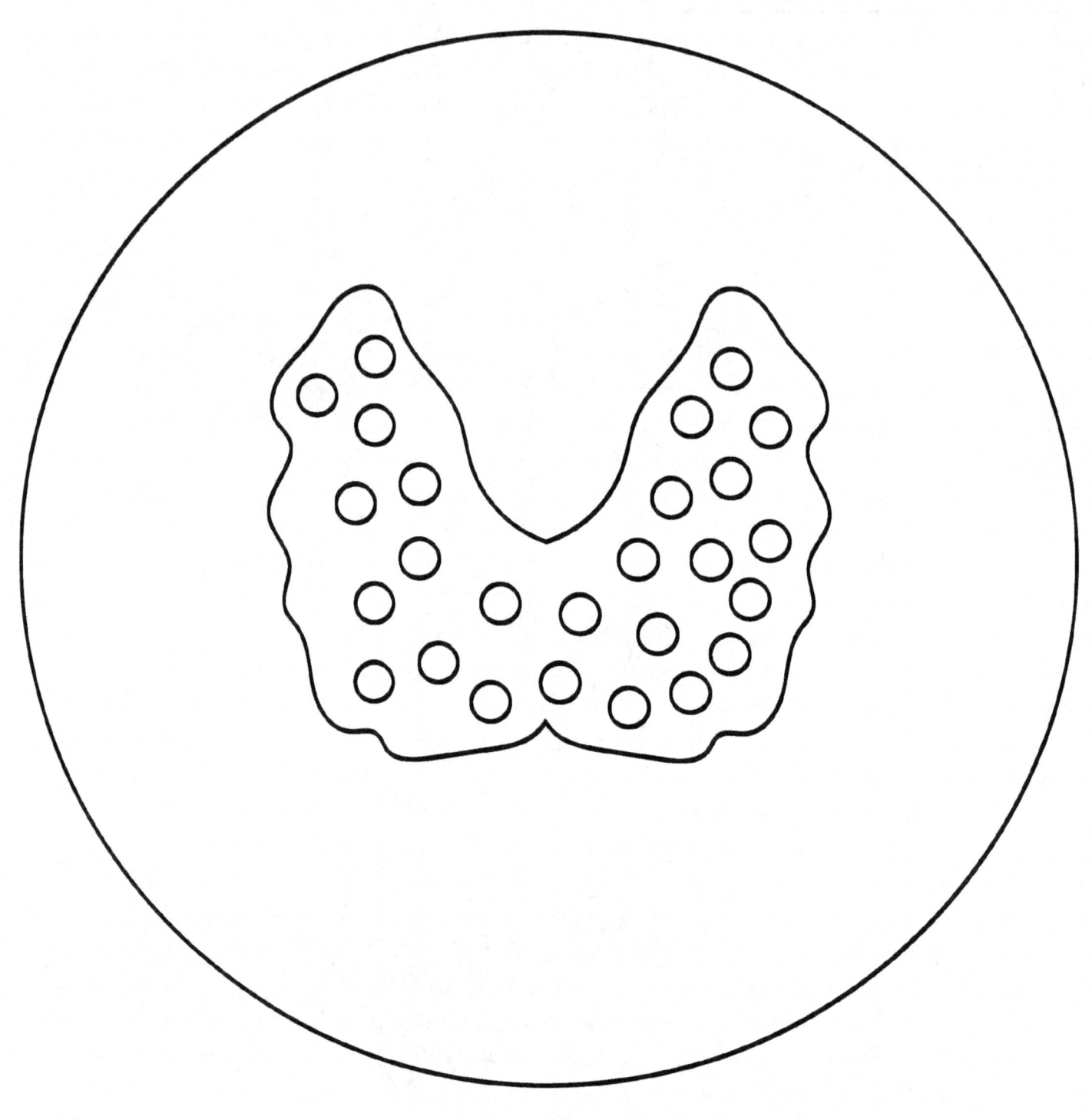

THYROID

I Can See

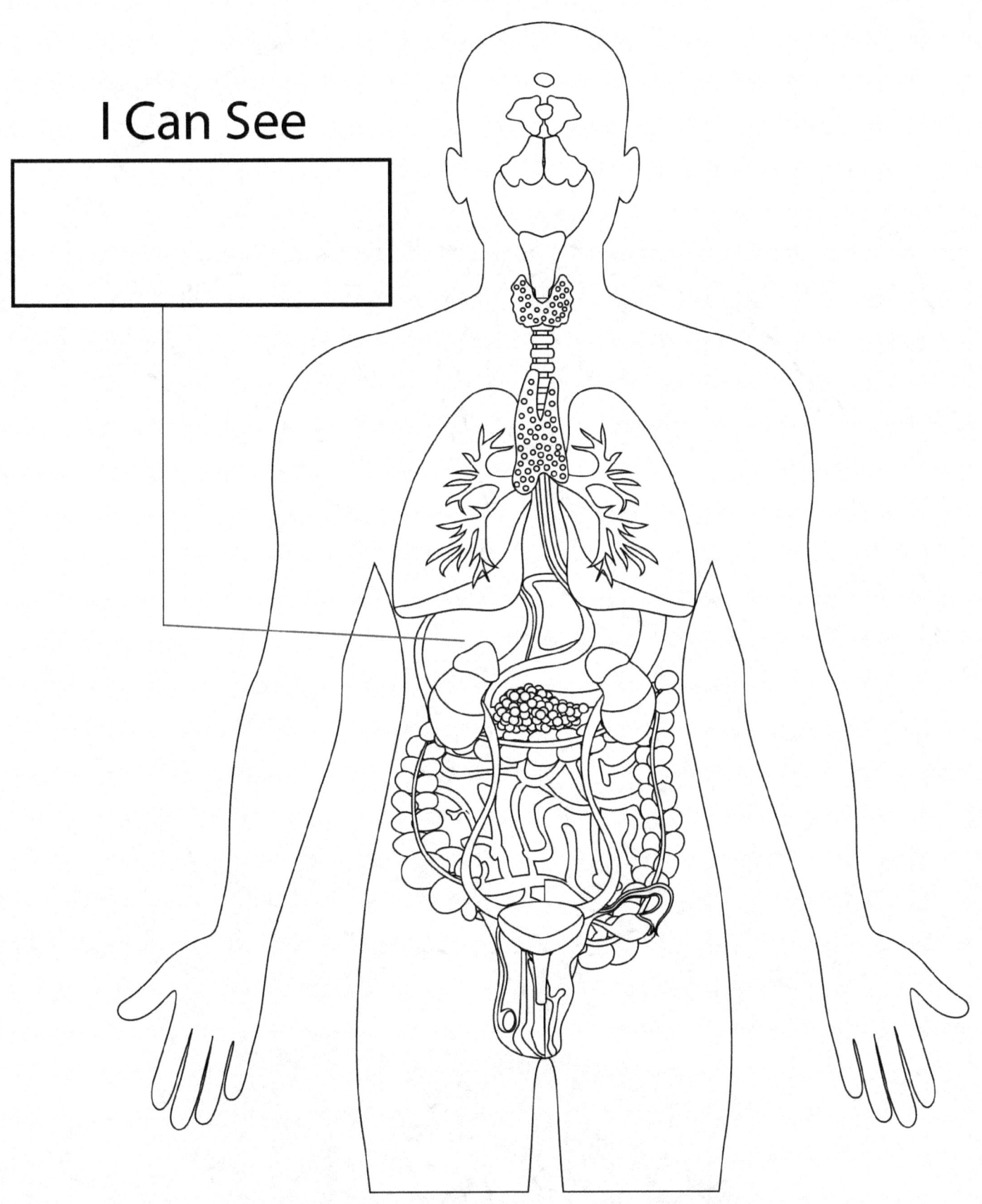

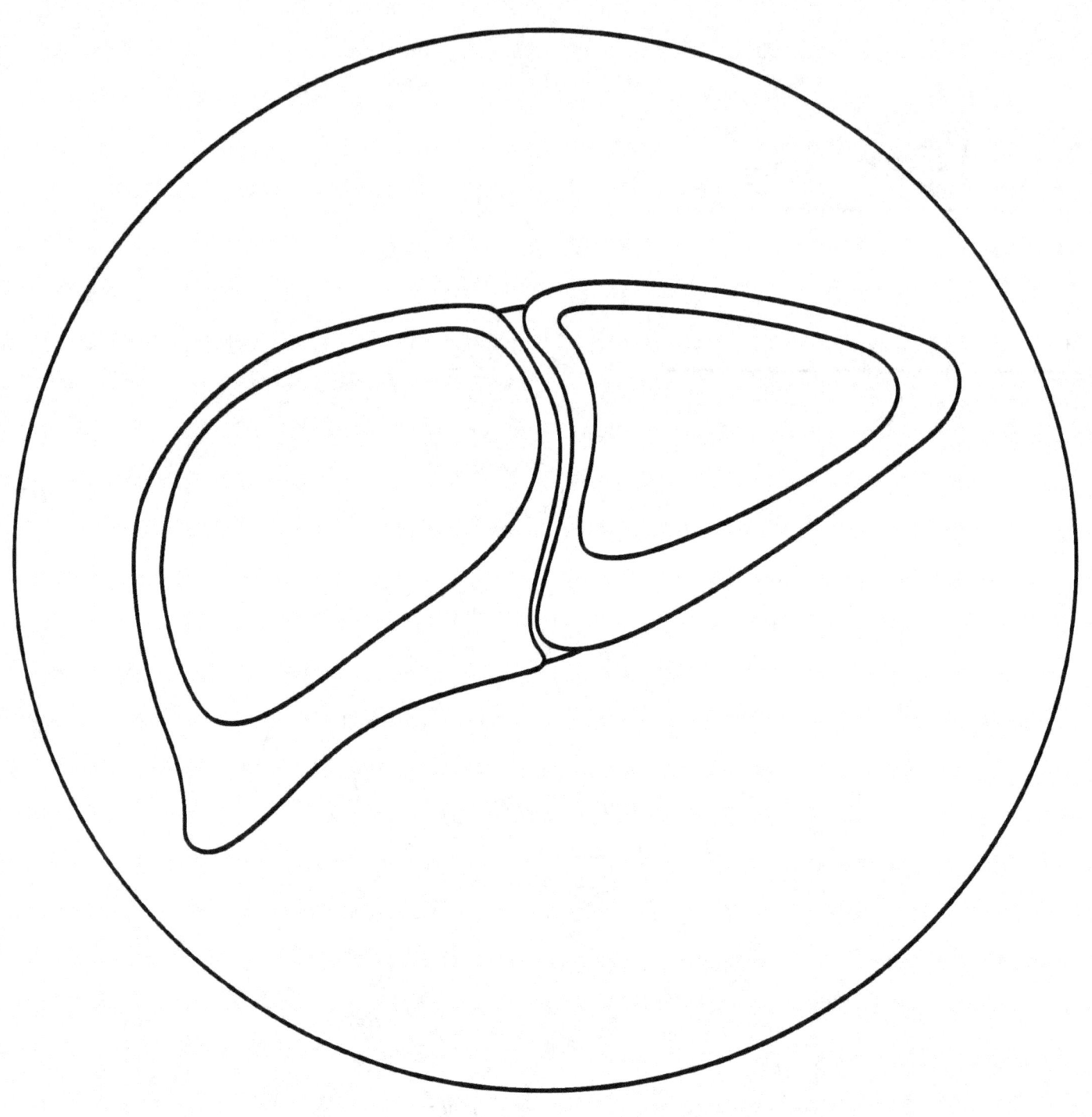

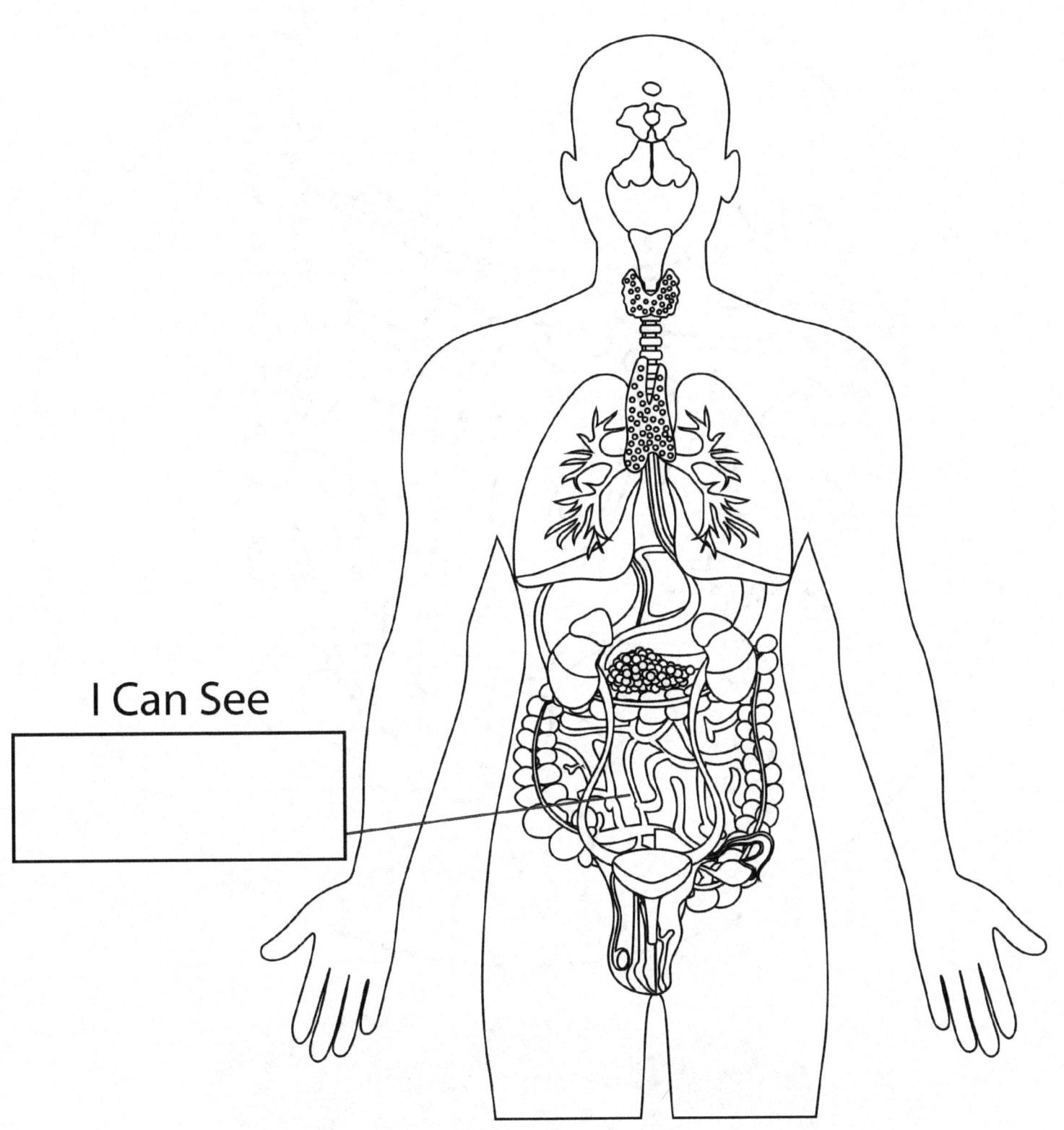

I Can See

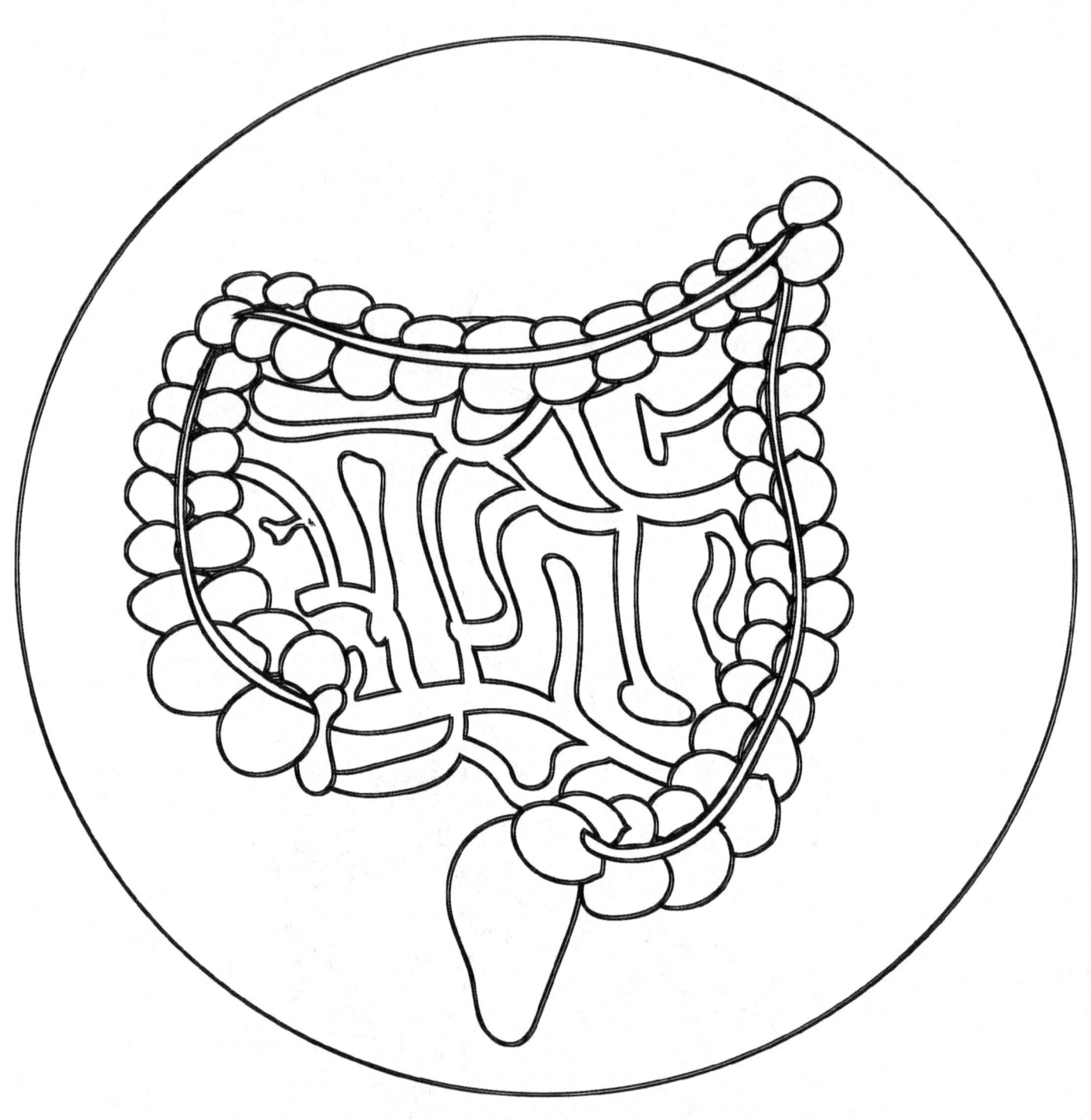

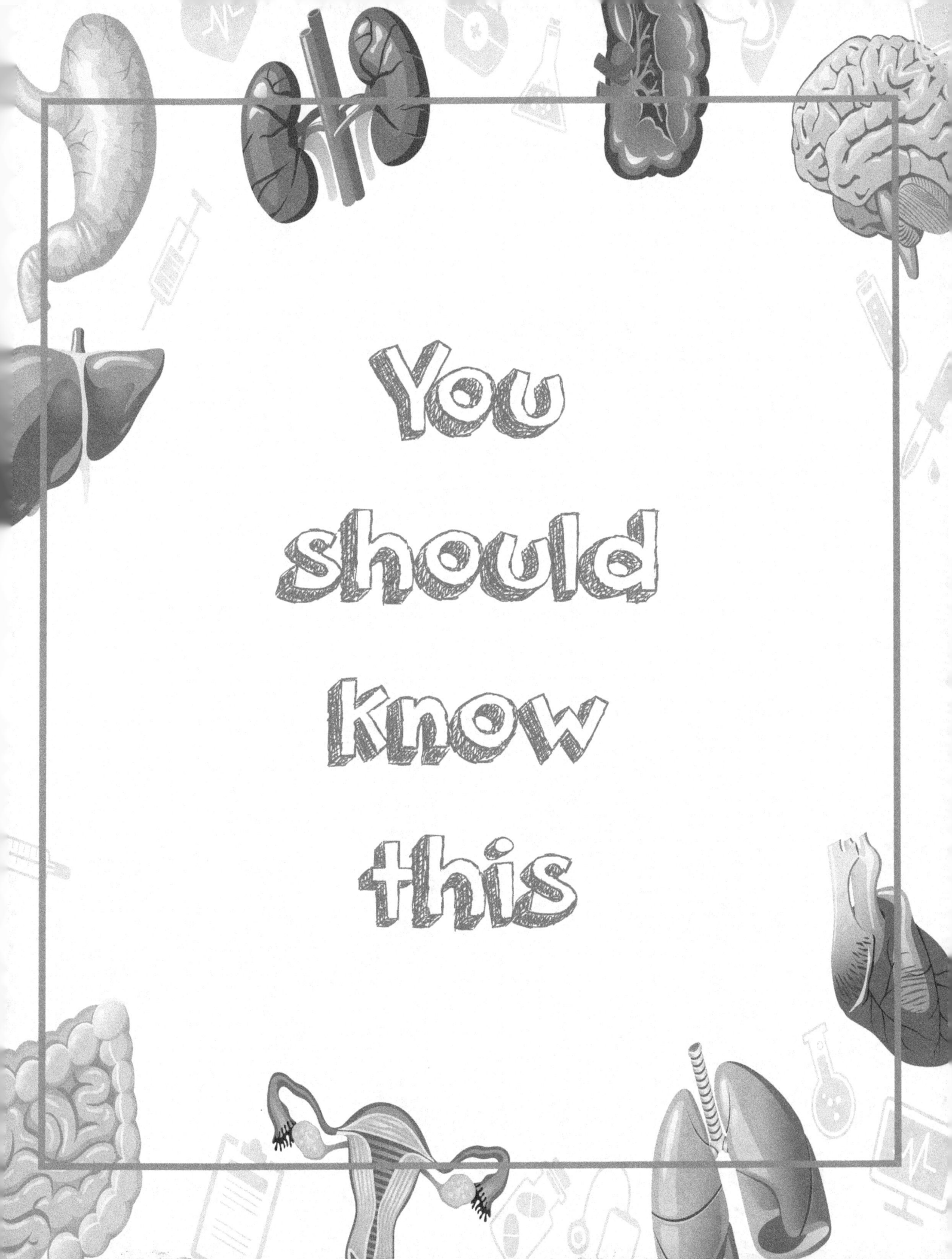

BRAIN

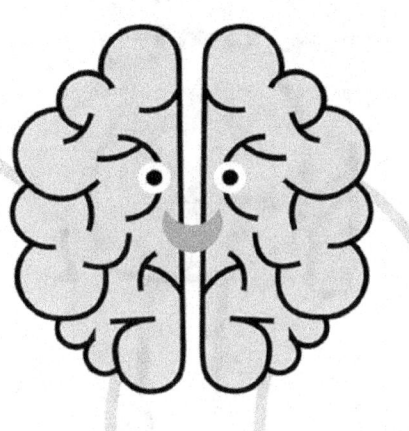

Your brain control all your movements, thoughts and decisions. It has billions of cells who receive information throughout your body. Eating healthy foods is important for your bain.

HEART

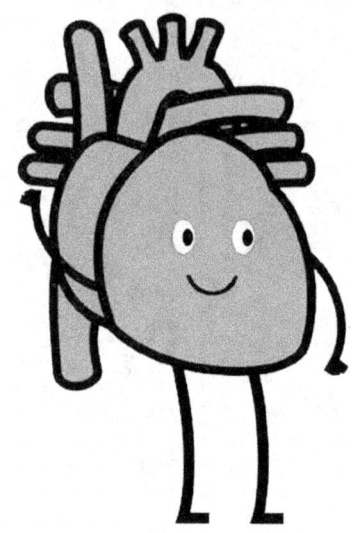

Your heart sends blood around your body. The blood provides your body with the oxygen and nutrients it needs.
Your heart is sort of like a pump made of muscles.
It's actually right in the middle of your chest between your two lungs.

LUNGS

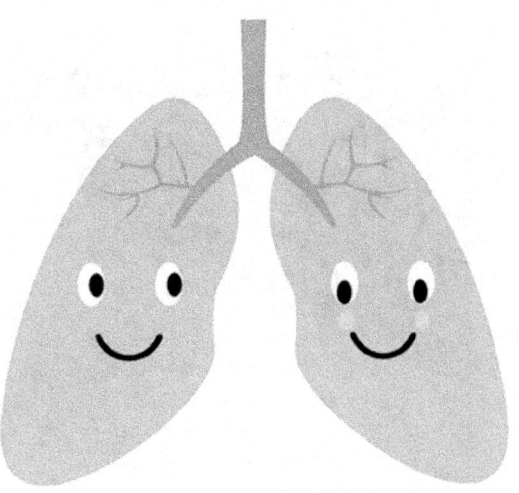

You have two lungs.
The lung on your left is a bit smaller than the lung on the right because it has to make room for your heart to fit in your chest too.
They work together with your heart to help you breath in and out.

LIVER

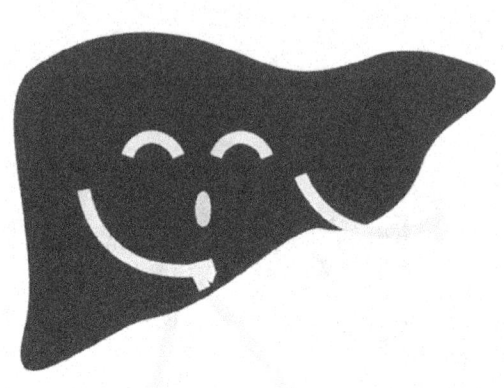

Your liver's main job is to clean your blood. It produces an important digestive liquid called bile.
Your liver is the largest solid organ in your body.
You cannot live without your liver.

STOMACH

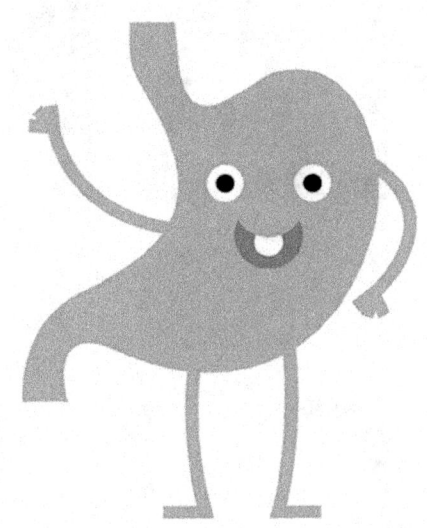

Your stomach a stretchy sack shaped like the letter J. Your stomach's job is to store the food you've eaten, to break down the food into a liquidy mixture, to slowly empty that liquidy mixture into the small intestine.

THANK YOU!

We hope you are happy with this book!

www.ingramcontent.com/pod-product-compliance
Lightning Source LLC
Chambersburg PA
CBHW060436220526
45465CB00008B/3165

www.ingramcontent.com/pod-product-compliance
Lightning Source LLC
Chambersburg PA
CBHW060436220526
45465CB00008B/3164